fair oaks 1862

mcclellan's peninsula campaign

ANGUS KONSTAM

fair oaks 1862

mcclellan's peninsula campaign

Praeger Illustrated Military History Series

PRAEGER

Westport, Connecticut
London

Library of Congress Cataloging-in-Publication Data

Konstam, Angus.
   Fair Oaks, 1862: McClellan's Peninsula Campaign / Angus Konstam.
      p. cm. – (Praeger illustrated military history, ISSN 1547-206X)
   Originally published: Oxford: Osprey, 2003
   Includes bibliographical references and index.
   ISBN 0-275-98449-4 (alk. paper)
   1. Fair Oaks, Battle of, Va., 1862. 2. Fair Oaks, Battle of, Va., 1862 – Pictorial works.
   I. Title. II. Series.
   E473.65.K66   2004
   973.7'32–dc22   2004050381

British Library Cataloguing in Publication Data is available.

First published in paperback in 2003 by Osprey Publishing Limited, Elms Court,
Chapel Way, Botley, Oxford OX2 9LP. All rights reserved.

Copyright © 2004 by Osprey Publishing Limited

Library of Congress Catalog Card Number: 2004050381
ISBN: 0-275-98449-4
ISSN: 1547-206X

Praeger Publishers, 88 Post Road West, Westport, CT 06881
An imprint of Greenwood Publishing Group, Inc.
www.praeger.com

Printed in China through World Print Ltd.

The paper used in this book complies with the Permanent Paper Standard issued
by the National Information Standards Organization (Z39.48-1984).

10 9 8 7 6 5 4 3 2 1

ILLUSTRATED BY: Steve Noon

CONTENTS

KEY TO MILITARY SYMBOLS

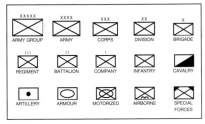

THE EASTERN THEATER, SPRING 1862

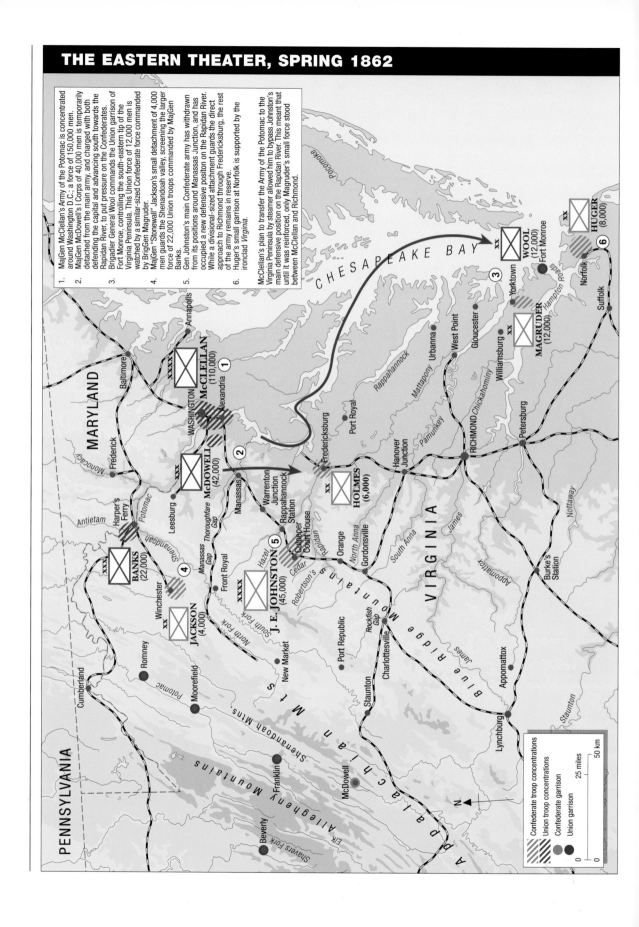

1. MajGen McClellan's Army of the Potomac is concentrated around Washington D.C.; a force of 150,000 men.

2. MajGen McDowell's I Corps of 40,000 men is temporarily detached from the main army, and charged with both defending the capital and advancing south towards the Rapidan River, to put pressure on the Confederates.

3. Brigadier General Wool commands the Union garrison of Fort Monroe, controlling the south-eastern tip of the Virginia Peninsula. This Union force of 12,000 men is watched by a similar-sized Confederate force commanded by BrigGen Magruder.

4. MajGen "Stonewall" Jackson's small detachment of 4,000 men guards the Shenandoah valley, screening the larger force of 22,000 Union troops commanded by MajGen Banks.

5. Gen Johnston's main Confederate army has withdrawn from its positions around Manassas Junction, and has occupied a new defensive position on the Rapidan River. While a divisional-sized attachment guards the direct approach to Richmond through Fredericksburg, the rest of the army remains in reserve.

6. Huger's small garrison at Norfolk is supported by the ironclad *Virginia*.

McClellan's plan to transfer the Army of the Potomac to the Virginia Peninsula by steamer allowed him to bypass Johnston's main defensive position on the Rapidan River. This meant that until it was reinforced, only Magruder's small force stood between McClellan and Richmond.

Map legend:
- Confederate troop concentrations
- Union troop concentrations
- Confederate garrison
- Union garrison

0   25 miles
0   50 km

Locations and forces shown on map:
- McCLELLAN (110,000)
- McDOWELL (42,000)
- BANKS (22,000)
- JACKSON (4,000)
- J. E. JOHNSTON (45,000)
- HOLMES (6,000)
- WOOL (12,000)
- MAGRUDER (12,000)
- HUGER (8,000)

Places: PENNSYLVANIA, MARYLAND, VIRGINIA, CHESAPEAKE BAY, Washington, Alexandria, Annapolis, Baltimore, Frederick, Harper's Ferry, Leesburg, Manassas, Warrenton Junction, Rappahannock Station, Culpeper Court House, Orange, Gordonsville, Charlottesville, Staunton, Lynchburg, Appomattox, Richmond, Petersburg, Fredericksburg, Hanover Junction, Port Royal, Urbanna, West Point, Gloucester, Williamsburg, Yorktown, Fort Monroe, Norfolk, Suffolk, Burke's Station, Winchester, Front Royal, New Market, Port Republic, Franklin, McDowell, Moorefield, Romney, Cumberland, Beverly, Hampton Roads

Rivers/features: Potomac, Shenandoah, Rappahannock, Mattapony, Pamunkey, Chickahominy, James, South Anna, North Anna, Rapidan, Cedar, Robertson's, Hazel, Nottaway, Appomattox, Monocacy, Antietam, Staunton, North Fork, South Fork, Blue Ridge Mountains, Shenandoah Mountains, Allegheny Mountains, Appalachian Mountains, Elk Mtns, Shavers Fork, Thoroughfare Gap, Manassas Gap, Rockfish Gap

INTRODUCTION

Across the great sweep of the Civil War, more attention has been paid to the climactic battles of Gettysburg, Chickamauga and even Chancellorsville than to the one battle that saved the Confederacy. The battle of Fair Oaks is best remembered as the action where the Confederate General Joseph E. Johnston was wounded, allowing President Jefferson Davis to appoint General Robert E. Lee to command the Southern army in Virginia. It has been portrayed as the battle that laid the groundwork for Lee's week-long campaign against Union General George B. McClellan, known as the Seven Days Battles, rather than a critical engagement in its own right. I hope to reestablish Fair Oaks, fought within sight of the Confederate capital of Richmond, as one of the key actions of the war. General McClellan's Army of the Potomac was a military leviathan designed to crush everything in its path. In the hands of a bold commander Richmond would have fallen before Confederate reinforcements arrived to defend the city. Instead, a combination of Union caution and Confederate deception allowed General Johnston to gather an army large enough to stand and fight. What followed was a confused, mismanaged but strategically crucial engagement fought between two commanders who were usually reluctant to risk battle. It was the battle that saved Richmond and along with it the Confederacy. With hindsight we can see that it also led to the

Strategic Impasse. This cartoon of Generals McClellan and Beauregard watching each other across the Potomac during the winter of 1861–62 summed up the situation in the Eastern Theater. McClellan was to encounter mounting criticism due to his apparent "masterly inactivity". (Library of Congress)

prolonging of the war by a little more than two and a half years, ending the notion of a Union victory using minimal force, and heralding the emrgence of "total war".

The origins of the campaign that led to the battle of Fair Oaks can be traced back almost a year to the summer of 1861. Following the Union defeat at the battle of First Manassas (also known as First Bull Run) in July, the Union Army of the Potomac was a demoralized force incapable of undertaking further offensive action against the Confederate army. Withdrawing to the banks of the Potomac, the Union army's camps clustered around Washington D.C. as if they sought protection from the capital rather than the other way round. Confederate cavalry patrols roamed within sight of the city, and politicians and civilians both feared an attack was imminent. At that crucial juncture General George B. McClellan arrived to take charge of the city's defenses. Already dubbed a hero by the Northern press after his success in a minor campaign in western Virginia, the man they called "Little Napoleon" seemed ideally suited to bring order from the chaos. He proved he was the man for the job, and within weeks a new confidence had spread through the Federal army, while President Lincoln and his fellow politicians were reassured that the enemy at the gates were unlikely to be marching down Pennsylvania Avenue in the foreseeable future.

With their base secure, McClellan and Lincoln began to plan a fresh offensive. When McClellan replaced the aging General Winfield Scott as Commander in Chief of the Union army, all restrictions on future operations seemed to have been removed. The first phase of the war, during which the North had imagined a mere show of force would be enough to bring the secessionists back into the fold, was clearly over. By the winter of 1861–62 the new policy was to force the Confederates to submit, while seeking to avoid unnecessary bloodshed or the destruction of the economic and social structure of the South. Initially, the President and his senior commander concurred on this approach. Lincoln became increasingly embroiled in Republican Party politics, however, and needed to appease the extremists (Radicals) within his own ranks. These were the men who advocated "total war", an immediate end to slavery and a complete annihilation of the Southern way of life. Political policy and military strategy began to diverge, while the apparent inactivity of McClellan and his army invited criticism. As a result, Lincoln and his new and radical Secretary of War, Edwin Stanton, began to interfere in McClellan's strategic planning.

Lincoln and Stanton both favored a direct advance on Richmond, which ensured that the Army of the Potomac remained between Washington and the Confederate army. McClellan advocated an altogether more ambitious plan, moving the bulk of his army by steamer to land behind Johnston's army, forcing it to withdraw to defend Richmond. While ultimately McClellan was allowed to proceed with his plan, the force available for the outflanking movement was reduced as both Lincoln and Stanton insisted a strong force remain in northern Virginia to defend Washington. The compromise meant that while McClellan's force was superior to that available to Johnston, he lacked the overwhelming superiority in numbers that would guarantee victory with a minimum of fighting. This political sabotage reinforced McClellan's tendency towards caution, and ultimately led to the failure of the Peninsula Campaign.

The movement of a force of 112,000 men from Washington to the tip of the Tidewater Peninsula altered the strategic balance in the theater, as initially less than 17,000 Confederates stood between McClellan and Richmond. Only the Union commander's caution in front of Yorktown and Williamsburg allowed Johnston time to rush reinforcements to the area, and to gather enough men to defend the capital. This said, he could do little to stop the Union advance, and by late May the Army of the Potomac was less than ten miles from its objective. The brilliant campaign conducted by General "Stonewall" Jackson in the Shenandoah Valley forced McClellan to halt operations while troops were diverted to northern Virginia. This delay left the Army of the Potomac in an awkward position, its force split by the marshy Chickahominy River. The normally cautious General Johnston saw an opportunity to strike the enemy, destroying a portion of the Union army in detail before it could be reinforced. The scene was set for the battle of Fair Oaks (also known as Seven Pines); a fight that pitted two inexperienced armies in a struggle that would decide the fate of Richmond. Confederate failure would almost inevitably mean the loss of the Confederate capital. Union defeat would shatter the dream of ending the war at a stroke by capturing Richmond. With such high stakes, it is little wonder that the ensuing battle was the bloodiest engagement fought thus far in the Eastern Theater, a slaughter on a new and alarming scale.

ORIGINS OF THE CAMPAIGN

On 26 July 1861, General George B. McClellan arrived in Washington. Five days before, the Union army of General Irvin A. McDowell had been comprehensively defeated at the battle of First Manassas (Bull Run), fought less than 25 miles west of the Union capital. Stragglers were still crossing the Potomac River into the city as McClellan assumed command of a shattered army. He was lucky in that, unlike his predecessor, McDowell, McClellan enjoyed the full support of both the press and the President. He also had a highly developed belief in his own abilities. A week after his arrival, McClellan submitted a general plan of operations, developed from an earlier proposal he had sent to General Winfield Scott, commander of all Union forces. While Scott's "Anaconda Plan" was essentially an economic strategy for war on the Confederacy, and involved a naval blockade and the capture of the Mississippi River, McClellan's plan favored the concentration of resources in a single thrust in overwhelming strength against the Confederate capital at Richmond. Both stratagems were based on the desire to end the war with minimum casualties, and to inflict minimal damage on the resources and people of the secessionist states. The manpower for this vast army was already being called to the colors, as President Lincoln requested the enlistment of 300,000 men for service in the Eastern Theater, with an additional 150,000 men earmarked for the West. As McClellan himself put it, the aim of a Union invasion of Virginia in overwhelming numbers would be "to reestablish the power of the Government and restore peace to the citizens in the shortest possible time." While the President and his advisors questioned the need for such a large-scale offensive, he did nothing to stand in McClellan's way. At this stage, the small Pennsylvanian general had complete control over the

Union transports at the quayside in Alexandria, Virginia, across the Potomac River from Washington D.C. General McClellan's ability to transport his army by steamer gave him an immense strategic advantage over his Confederate opponents. (Stratford Archive)

fate of his country. He was being given the resources and manpower needed to finish the war in a single bold stroke. His power increased on 1 November 1861, when General Winfield Scott retired, after undue pressure from both McClellan and Lincoln. During this time "Little Napoleon" (or "Little Mac" to his subordinates) had been busy improving the defenses of the capital, incorporating this new influx of manpower into the army, and ensuring that this new force had the equipment and resources it required. The one thing he did not contemplate was offensive action. McClellan's real gift as a general was not his skill on the battlefield but his administrative ability. It was McClellan who created the Army of the Potomac, and who turned it into a military tool capable of performing its strategic objective of overwhelming the enemy in Virginia. Unfortunately, it would be another two years before the army gained a commander capable of using it in the way McClellan had originally envisaged.

Across the Potomac, the Confederate army was well aware of the new spirit in Washington. General P.G.T. Beauregard was transferred from the theater, leaving General Joseph E. Johnston to face any advance by the Union Army of the Potomac. Although Johnston's advanced outpost at Falls Church was within seven miles of the Long Bridge crossing the Potomac into Washington, he was reluctant to risk any offensive action. Like McClellan, Johnston preferred to win campaigns through maneuver rather than open battle, and he was well aware that the enemy heavily outnumbered his 40,000 men. On 19 October, he abandoned his outposts and withdrew to Centreville, shortening his supply lines but reducing the pressure on Washington. His outposts north and southwest of Washington remained in place. While Union scouts cautiously advanced to occupy the abandoned Confederate positions around Fairfax Courthouse, a division commanded by Major General Charles P. Stone engaged in "a demonstration" against the Confederate position near Leesburg. Although Stone was an experienced and capable officer, some of his subordinates were neither. On 21 October, Colonel Edward Baker's brigade of Stone's division crossed the Potomac in a rash attack on a Confederate camp, but ran into the brigade of General Nathan G. Evans at Ball's Bluff. Evans drove the enemy back to the foot of a high cliff, and then destroyed Baker's command. The inexperienced Baker was killed during the battle, along with most of his men. The disaster prompted a political search for a scapegoat and, to avoid undue criticism, McClellan opted to sacrifice Stone to the Radical politicians who would otherwise cast the blame on the army commander. Stone was duly cashiered and imprisoned, an early casualty in McClellan's fight for survival.

For all his posturing McClellan was no fighting general. The debacle at Ball's Bluff, combined with inaccurate estimates of Confederate strength, led him to abandon plans for any offensive before the following spring. Despite increasing criticism of his apparent inactivity, "Little Mac" refused to be drawn into any precipitous action. His advisors did not help him. His headquarters included an intelligence section, staffed by civilians from the Pinkerton Detective Agency. Unused to dealing with military intelligence, they consistently overestimated Confederate numbers, and McClellan made the mistake of believing their reports. Consequently, while his own forces significantly outnumbered the Confederates, McClellan believed the reverse was true. President Lincoln was forced to defend his senior commander, but "Little Mac" did not endear himself to his Commander in Chief, refusing to include Lincoln in his plans. When Lincoln wrote to McClellan on 1 December proposing a particular strategy, the general responded ten days later with a letter that mentioned, "*another plan of campaign that I do not think at all anticipated by the enemy.*" Without a doubt, this was the first reference to the strategic plan that would lead to the Peninsula Campaign. He felt no need to expand on his idea, and continued to exclude the President from his strategic planning, which increasingly led Lincoln to distrust McClellan. When the plan was eventually aired, Lincoln opposed it, as he felt it left Washington vulnerable to attack. McClellan felt that a Union army near Richmond would force the Confederates to withdraw south to

During the skirmish at Ball's Bluff, Virginia, on 21 October 1861, Colonel Nathan Evans and his Confederate brigade routed a superior force of Union troops. This engraving shows the unsuccessful advance of the 15th Massachusetts Volunteer Infantry during the engagement. The regiment suffered heavy casualties during the fighting. (Library of Congress)

Ball's Bluff, near Leesburg, Virginia provided McClellan's reorganized Army of the Potomac with its baptism of fire. The operation was a disaster, as Confederate troops lined the top of these bluffs and fired on the Union troops trapped below them. (Stratford Archive)

defend their own capital, so removing the threat to the Union one. This growing distrust was fuelled by the appointment of Edwin Stanton as Secretary of War. The consummate politician, Stanton hid his dislike of both Lincoln and McClellan, but worked hard to drive a wedge between the two men. To Stanton, McClellan was "*not a good Union man*" as he was not a strong abolitionist, and lacked an intense dislike of Southerners. Worse still, the general was a Democrat. Stanton therefore tried to strip McClellan of as much power as possible, partly by encouraging Lincoln to intervene in military affairs, and he encouraged public criticism of the general.

On 27 January 1862, McClellan opened the paper and read that the President had issued General Order No. 1, stating that the Army of the Potomac would advance against the enemy on 22 February, which was Washington's birthday. On 31 January, Lincoln followed this up with Special Order No. 1, which went so far as to specify the roads the army was to advance down. Clearly McClellan could not accept this kind of interference without a fight. On 3 February, he sent the President a letter, outlining his own plan to bypass Confederate resistance by conducting an amphibious landing behind Confederate lines. He also listed all the reasons a frontal assault against the Confederate position would not work. His plan was to seize the small Virginian tobacco port of Urbanna, on the south side of the Rappahannock estuary. He would then be behind the Confederate army and a mere 50 miles from Richmond. With naval support he would develop a supply base, then drive south towards the Confederate capital. Lincoln did not respond to McClellan's letter, but he was openly concerned at the prospect of leaving Washington exposed to attack. Over the next few weeks, Stanton continued to undermine both McClellan and the new plan. The crisis came to a head on 8 March when Lincoln held a frank private meeting with McClellan. During this, the President told his senior general that some politicians had described McClellan's plan to leave Washington unprotected as "traitorous". "Little Mac" was furious, and retorted that

The occupation of Fort Monroe and its hinterland by General Wool and 10,000 Union troops gave McClellan a secure base of operations, even though Wool and his men were not considered under "Little Mac's" command. (Stratford Archive)

he would call together his senior officers, and let them vote on the efficacy of the Urbanna plan. Sure enough, the meeting was held later that morning, and McClellan's officers discussed the plan before the general let them vote. Edwin Sumner, Irvin McDowell, Samuel Heintzelman and the Chief Engineer John Barnard voted against it. The remaining eight, including Fitz-John Porter and Erasmus Keyes supported McClellan's plan. When the cabal reported to the President, Lincoln was forced to agree to McClellan's scheme. "Little Mac" had won the support he needed, but his victory would be short-lived.

The next round of presidential interference came that afternoon, when Lincoln ordered that the Army of the Potomac be organized into four army corps, led by generals appointed by the administration rather than by McClellan. While "Little Mac" railed against this interference, with the exception of Keyes, the commanders Lincoln chose were ones whom McClellan had already selected for higher command. At the same time the President set the date of the start of the spring campaign as 18 March, but added that the army needed to ensure that Washington was adequately protected before any advance began. Under Stanton's influence, Lincoln added that the size of Washington's garrison be determined by "the general in chief and the commanders of army corps." In effect, McClellan was being forced to command by consensus. These decisions were ratified as Presidential Order No. 2. To someone with McClellan's ego, this represented an intolerable level of interference, but he was left with little room to maneuver.

Confederate commander General Johnston was aware that a Union attack was imminent, and on 8 March, he began pulling his forces south towards Fredericksburg, on the Rappahannock. The town was located midway between Washington and Richmond, behind an easily defensible river. More significantly for McClellan, it was also closer to Urbanna, which was now only slightly behind Confederate lines, and Johnston could probably march to contain McClellan's bridgehead before enough Union troops could be brought ashore to drive on Richmond. On the same day, the Confederate ironclad *Virginia* sortied from Norfolk into Hampton Roads and destroyed two blockading warships[1]. Although the arrival of the

Union troops unloading supplies onto the wharf at Fort Monroe, at the tip of the Tidewater Peninsula. McClellan initially rejected this as a landing site as he considered it to be too far from the Confederate capital. (Stratford Archive)

Union ironclad *Monitor* the following day ultimately countered the threat from the Confederate ironclad, these two developments forced McClellan to consider an alternative to his Urbanna plan. Meanwhile, he gave orders for his army to march out of their encampments and occupy the abandoned Confederate defenses around Centerville. McClellan had no real desire to catch Johnston, only to reap the reward of securing the enemy positions that had posed a threat to Washington. This achieved, he called a council of war to review his options. When he first considered an amphibious landing, McClellan had considered landing at Fort Monroe rather than Urbanna, but abandoned the idea as he considered the Union enclave to be too far from the Confederate capital. Then, on 12 March, McClellan read in the newspaper that he was no longer the Commander in Chief of the Union Army. Lincoln's General Order No. 3 issued the previous day stated that McClellan was responsible only for the Army of the Potomac, and that all other forces were answerable directly to Edwin Stanton. This also meant that McClellan no longer had any authority over other formations in the Shenandoah Valley or the Washington area. "Little Mac" recognized he was being stripped of power and realized that only immediate action gave him the chance to regain control of the army from Stanton. Consequently, during the afternoon of 12 March, he held his second council of war. Present were the four men who had voted against his Urbanna plan four days earlier. This time McClellan won them round, and they unanimously agreed on a new, even more ambitious venture. The Army of the Potomac would move by water to Fort Monroe, then advance towards Richmond up Virginia's Tidewater Peninsula. The group also agreed to detach a force of 25,000 men, which would remain near Centerville to defend Washington. Lincoln and Stanton were informed of the decision that evening, while McClellan spoke to the press, telling them that at long last he was ready to unleash his army. Therefore, on 13 March, after six days of political and military uncertainty, "Little Mac" regained the initiative and the campaign of 1862 got under way.

---

1 See Campaign 103 *Hampton Roads 1862 – First clash of the Ironclads*

CHRONOLOGY

1861

10 June Skirmish at Big Bethel, in the peninsula.
21 July Union defeat at the battle of Manassas (Bull Run).
26 July General McClellan takes over command of the Army around Washington.
19 October Confederates withdraw to entrenchments around Centerville.
21 October Union defeat at Ball's Bluff.
11 December McClellan makes his first reference to a plan to bypass the enemy and strike behind him.

1862

February Mounting criticism of McClellan's inaction in the Union press and in the government. Transports and stores are gathered at Alexandria for the new campaign.
3 February McClellan outlines his plan for an amphibious landing at Urbanna in a letter to President Lincoln.
8 March Lincoln and McClellan hold a stormy meeting, where McClellan is accused of leaving Washington undefended. He responds by calling a council of war. McClellan's plan is ratified by a majority of his senior commanders. Four Union Army Corps are created (I–IV). Confederate withdrawal from Centerville to Fredericksburg begins.
8–9 March Battle of Hampton Roads. CSS *Virginia* threatens to destroy the Union blockading squadron at Hampton Roads, but arrival of USS *Monitor* leads to an indecisive battle, and naval stand-off.
10 March Union troops occupy Centerville.
11 March McClellan demoted from Commander in Chief of the Union Army to Commander of the Army of the Potomac. Secretary of War Edwin Stanton assumes responsibility for grand strategy.
12 March McClellan's second council of war held in Centerville approves his plan to land the army at Fort Monroe.
16 March Johnston establishes his new headquarters in Fredericksburg.
17 March Army of the Potomac begins embarking on transports at Alexandria, Virginia.
23 March Battle of Kernstown, in the Shenandoah Valley.
24 March Union forces begin disembarking at Fort Monroe.
2 April McClellan lands at Fort Monroe.
3 April Johnston marches his army from Fredericksburg to Richmond.
4 April Union advance up the peninsula begins.
5 April Keyes' IV Corps encounters Magruder's defenses along the Warwick River. Skirmish at Lee's Mill. Heintzelman's III Corps approaches Yorktown.
6 April Sumner's II Corps lands near Fort Monroe, and joins advance. McClellan overestimates strength of Confederate defenses. Advanced units of Johnston's army parade through Richmond to raise morale.
7 April McClellan decides to initiate formal siege of Yorktown.
14 April President Davis holds council of war in Richmond.
16 April Union troops probe across Warwick River.
30 April McClellan announces his siege preparations are nearly complete.
3 May Confederates abandon Yorktown and retire up the peninsula.
4 May Yorktown occupied by Union troops, and then opened up as a supply base.
5 May Battle of Williamsburg. Longstreet protects rear of Johnston's army.
7 May Union troops land at Eltham's Landing on the York River.
9 May Norfolk abandoned as General Huger is recalled to defend Richmond.
11 May The CSS *Virginia* is destroyed by her crew, opening lower James River to the Union fleet.

15 May Union ironclads repulsed by Confederate batteries at Drewry's Bluff.

16 May McClellan establishes new supply base at the White House, on the York River.

17 May McClellan informed that McDowell's force will reinforce his army.

18 May McClellan creates two new army Corps (V–VI).

20 May McClellan probes south of the Chickahominy.

23 May Battle of Front Royal, in the Shenandoah Valley.

24 May Keyes' IV Corps moves into positions around Seven Pines. McDowell recalled to defend northern Virginia.

25 May Heintzelman's III Corps sent across Chickahominy to hold line of White Oak Swamp. Second Battle of Winchester, in the Shenandoah Valley.

27 May Skirmish at Hanover Court House.

29 May Johnston orders his divisions to concentrate their forces in front of Richmond.

30 May Heavy storm hits the battle area, flooding the Chickahominy River. Johnston gives orders to launch attack the following day.

31 May Battle of Fair Oaks

4.00am Longstreet's and D.H. Hill's divisions advance towards Union positions.

6.00 Scheduled start time of Confederate attack. Whiting's Division reaches its jump-off position at Old Church.

9.00 Longstreet's Division marches from Gillies Creek to Williamsburg Road.

10.00 Johnston becomes aware that Longstreet has taken wrong road.

11.00 D.H. Hill's Division reaches its jump-off position on Williamsburg Road.

1.00pm Whiting's Division reaches advanced positions on Nine Mile Road. D.H. Hill begins his attack.

1.20 Garland and Anderson attack Naglee's Brigade west of Seven Pines.

1.40 Rodes attacks Palmer's Brigade, supported by Rains.

2.00 Sumner's II Corps prepares to cross the Chickahominy to help Keyes.

2.10 Casey's Division breaks, and Rodes captures Casey's Redoubt.

2.30 Union routers reach safety of second Union line, held by Couch's Division.

3.00 D.H. Hill launches attacks on Union line, but all assaults are repulsed.

4.00 Berry's Brigade of Kearny's Division arrives to support Union line. Johnston orders Whiting to attack down Nine Mile Road.

4.15 Union attacks against D.H. Hill's right flank are repulsed.

4.30 Sedgwick's Division approaches the Adams House.

4.40 R.H. Anderson re-invigorates Confederate offensive by attacking Couch's right flank.

5.00 Sumner joins Sedgwick as his troops form a solid defensive position.

5.15 Whiting launches his first attack against Sedgwick's position.

5.20 Couch's position is taken as Union defenders retire to the third line of defense.

5.40 Whiting uses Hatton's Brigade to launch a second attack, which is repulsed.

6.00 Whiting calls off his attack as Johnston arrives on the field.

6.15 D.H. Hill and Longstreet probe eastwards towards the third Union line.

7.00 Johnston is seriously wounded, and carried from the battlefield. Smith assumes command of the Confederate army.

7.15 Fighting dies out along the Williamsburg Road, but skirmishing continues.

8.45 Dusk brings an end to the fighting.

Virginia's Tidewater Peninsula was mostly devoid of large towns and railroads. Instead, a network of secondary roads linked a string of small hamlets between Hampton and Richmond. This is New Kent Court House, a small hamlet on the Williamsburg Road, south of the Pamunkey River. This sketch of the hamlet was made on 19 May 1862. (Stratford Archive)

During the night both sides re-arrange their lines. Sumner and Heintzelman form the Union front line, while Keyes' shattered Corps is withdrawn to the rear. Similarly D.H Hill's division in the south and Whiting's in the north are placed in the Confederate reserve, while Huger's Division is brought forward to reinforce Longstreet's Division.

1 June Battle of Fair Oaks (Second Day)

1.00am Smith and Longstreet meet to plan the day's battle.

5.40 Dawn.

6.00 Hood's Brigade engages in firefight with Dana's Brigade near Fair Oaks.

6.30 D.H. Hill orders Pickett to advance into the woods to the north.

7.00 Hooker orders his division to advance.

7.10 Pickett encounters Birney's Brigade, and a vicious firefight ensues.

7.15 D.H. Hill orders Mahone and Armistead to advance to relieve Pickett.

7.25 Mahone contacts French's Brigade, driving it back in disorder.

7.45 Howard's Brigade enters the fray, pinning Armistead.

8.00 Wilcox and Pryor repulse Hooker's attacks.

8.10 Howard leads a force into a gap in the Confederate line, but is wounded.

8.30 The Union line retires as far as the railroad, but Mahone's Brigade breaks.

8.40 Pickett retires, to avoid being completely cut off.

9.00 D.H. Hill authorizes a general withdrawal to the Seven Pines position.

9.20 The Union troops around the Williamsburg Road break off their pursuit.

2 June R.E. Lee assumes command of the Confederate Army.

3 June Confederate Army officially designated the Army of Northern Virginia.

4 June McClellan orders his troops to entrench along their front.

8 June Battle of Cross Keys, in the Shenandoah.

9 June Battle of Port Republic, in the Shenandoah.

10 June Lee orders BrigGen J.E.B. Stuart to probe the Union right flank.

12–15 June J.E.B. Stuart rides around the Army of the Potomac.

23 June Jackson visits Richmond to confer with Lee.

24 June Lee gives orders that will initiate the Seven Days Battles.

OPPOSING PLANS

THE CAMPAIGN

The basic premise of General McClellan's plan was very simple. To him, the best way to defend Washington was to attack Richmond. If their capital was threatened, McClellan argued, the Confederates would pull back every available man to defend Richmond. With the exception of the York and James rivers, the Union had control of the inland waterways of the Chesapeake basin. This meant that not only could they land troops virtually anywhere they wanted, they could also provide them with naval gunfire support, and could supply the troops with provisions and reinforcements. It was the same basic premise which lay behind British strategic thinking during the American Revolutionary War almost a century before.

When General Joseph Johnston's Confederate army withdrew from its entrenchments around Centerville to its new positions at Fredericksburg, it removed any direct threat to Washington. In order to advance towards the Potomac, the Confederates would have to rebuild the railroads of Northern Virginia that had been destroyed during their retreat. This would buy time for troops such as General Banks' command to move into position to defend the Union capital. The Confederate withdrawal therefore reduced the need for a large body of troops to remain in the Manassas area, allowing McClellan to concentrate his forces for a decisive thrust towards Richmond.

The Confederate withdrawal also ended plans for McClellan's landing at Urbanna. Throughout February and early March, transports had been gathered to move the Army of the Potomac southwards down the Chesapeake. McClellan was determined that this valuable strategic resource would not be wasted. Consequently a new amphibious landing was planned on the tip of the Tidewater Peninsula. Fort Monroe was built to defend the anchorage of Hampton Roads, but by early 1862 it served as a useful Union toe-hold on the Virginia coast. Its guns protected the anchorage, and together with the ironclad USS *Monitor*, they were deemed powerful enough to keep the Confederate ironclad CSS *Virginia* at bay. The fort and its immediate hinterland were defended by 12,000 Union troops, commanded by General Wool, an elderly but experienced officer. Wool estimated that Confederate forces in the peninsula amounted to no more than 15,000 men, a force that was considered no match for the Army of the Potomac. Although little could be done about the CSS *Virginia*, the US Navy claimed that with army support they could neutralize the Confederate gun positions at Yorktown and across the river at Gloucester Point, and so open up the York River. This could then be used as a secure supply route, ensuring that the Army of the Potomac would want for nothing as it advanced up

General John B. Magruder (nicknamed "Prince John" because of his lavish lifestyle) may have lacked the flair for command shown by other Confederate generals, but his actions around Yorktown in April 1862 helped shape the course of the Peninsula Campaign. (Virginia War Museum, Newport News, VA)

RIGHT **Richmond, Virginia: the capital of the Confederacy, and McClellan's objective in the summer of 1862. He thought that if the city could be captured by overwhelming force, the Confederacy would collapse. (Stratford Archive)**

the peninsula. On paper it was a perfect plan. Unfortunately, it failed to take into account faulty Union intelligence, the weather, the largely unmapped ground the troops would march over, and the resourcefulness of the Confederates opposing them. It also did not allow for the possibility of interference from Washington.

Within hours of landing, McClellan learned that a quarter of his army was no longer available to him, as it was retained near Manassas to defend Washington. The force that remained was still sufficiently large to crush the Confederate force holding the peninsula, but caution, over-estimation of enemy strength and inertia led to lengthy delays. Consequently it took over a month for the Army of the Potomac to march from Fort Monroe to its positions outside Richmond, astride the Chickahominy River. This gave General Johnston the time he needed to gather his forces. Meanwhile General "Stonewall" Jackson's campaign in the Shenandoah Valley ensured that neither the Union troops near Manassas nor those in the Shenandoah would be able to join in the fighting around Richmond. Also, the possibility that McDowell's Corps of 42,000 men would march south and join forces with the rest of the army outside Richmond dictated McClellan's actions as he approached Richmond. He was forced to maintain forces on both sides of the Chickahominy River. Jackson helped ensure McDowell's reinforcements never reached McClellan. "Little Mac" was a brilliant organizer, and a strategist of some merit, but he was reluctant to risk his troops in battle. He always envisaged fighting a climactic "Waterloo-like" battle outside Richmond; an engagement fought on ground of his own choosing using all the forces he had at his disposal. He was still planning this final battle when General Johnston seized the initiative and attacked the Union army south of the Chickahominy.

Confederate strategy was equally simple. Joseph Johnston had already withdrawn his army to the Rappahannock when McClellan sailed south. John Magruder already had a small force in the peninsula, while

George B. McClellan proved to be a genius at organization, and transformed the Union Army into a well-equipped fighting force after the debacle at Manassas. Unfortunately, this administrative skill was not matched by a genius for battlefield command. (US Military Academy, West Point, NY)

Benjamin Huger protected Norfolk. Up in the Shenandoah, Lee had sent Thomas "Stonewall" Jackson to pin the Union forces in the area. If Johnston was to contain McClellan, he needed to move his army south while Magruder bought time for reinforcements to arrive. In the same way that McClellan was being viewed with suspicion by Lincoln, President Jefferson Davis was slowly losing confidence in Johnston. When Johnston retreated from Centerville to Fredericksburg, he did not inform the Confederate President, an act that Davis viewed as tantamount to willful disobedience. They also disagreed on strategy. Johnston was a defensive-minded general who disliked taking unnecessary chances. His stratagem to defend the peninsula was to delay the Army of the Potomac below Yorktown for as long as possible with whatever forces Magruder had at his disposal. Meanwhile Johnston would move his army to Richmond, and then strip the Confederate coastal garrisons to create an army that was large enough to stop McClellan. He could then attack McClellan outside Richmond, while the Union army was far from its supply centers, and well away from the rivers where the US Navy could provide it with gunfire support. President Davis and his military advisor General Robert E. Lee favored a reinforcement of Magruder, where Johnston would move all available troops to Magruder's position, then contest every mile of the peninsula.

To complicate matters, Johnston had as little control of those forces in Virginia not directly under his command as McClellan had over those around Washington and in the Shenandoah. It was Lee who controlled Confederate forces in the Shenandoah, on the coast near Norfolk and in central Virginia, a situation that made Johnston complain on 8 May "my authority does not extend beyond the troops immediately around me." Johnston was therefore forced into a fight in the central peninsula. Fortunately he had the military support of Lee, who diverted reinforcements and supplies to the peninsula by way of a compromise, gradually building up Johnston's strength so he could launch a counterattack against McClellan when the time came. The decision to abandon the Yorktown line and withdraw towards Richmond was a classic example of Johnston's defensive genius. He seemed to know intuitively when the enemy was about to launch an all-out attack, and he was able to withdraw just before the Union offensive began, catching McClellan off balance. He

Union strategy was hindered by the lack of topographical information available to the planners. For example, the Chickahominy River (shown here near the site of Grapevine Bridge) presented a far greater obstacle than the strategists first imagined. (Author's photograph)

then fell back upon his supply base at Richmond, where reinforcements and munitions were waiting for him to launch his own offensive.

THE BATTLE

McClellan might have been a strategist, but he was no tactician. At the end of May 1862, his army was split by the Chickahominy River, leaving either wing vulnerable to attack. There were several reasons for this curious disposition of forces. First, McClellan imagined that he was about to be reinforced by General McDowell's I Corps (now known as the Department of the Rappahannock), marching south towards Richmond from Centerville. Consequently, of the five Army Corps at his disposal, three were arrayed on the northern side of the Chickahominy River, where they were in a position to join forces with McDowell. He also wanted to keep two Corps on the southern side of the river, as they occupied the ground from which McClellan eventually planned to launch his final drive on Richmond. These dispositions took no account of the relative size of his five Corps. The selection had more to do with army politics than with strategy. Of the four Corps commanders created just before the campaign got under way, three (McDowell, Sumner, and Heintzelman) had voted against McClellan's Urbanna plan. McClellan also viewed Keyes with suspicion. These men had all been senior to him before the war began, and they were therefore less likely to blindly follow their commander's strategy than others in the army. On 18 May, McClellan created two new provisional Army Corps (V and VI), giving command of them to a pair of trusted subordinates: Fitz-John Porter and William B. Franklin. To create them he stripped his existing three Corps of some of their best troops. In effect, he created an elite force that had the pick of men and supplies, and which was staffed by generals he could trust. Although McDowell's order to march towards McClellan was rescinded by Edwin Stanton on 24 May, McClellan hoped the cancellation would be overturned, and consequently

The Army of the Potomac had to commit considerable effort and resources to the supply of its soldiers in the Tidewater Peninsula. In this view of the approach to Grapevine Bridge over the Chickahominy River, a "corduroy" road of felled logs has been laid over a raised trestle approach road to the river. (Library of Congress)

he retained three Corps, or six divisions' in position to support McDowell on the north bank of the Chickahominy River. As he saw this as the decisive sector, he concentrated his new divisions there. Porter's V Corps and Franklin's VI Corps were placed in the Union van, behind Beaver Dam Creek. The less politically reliable Sumner (II Corps) was also north of the river, but kept in the rear. To the south of the Chickahominy, Keyes' IV Corps was deployed astride the Seven Pines crossroads, with one division behind the other along the Williamsburg Road. Heintzelman's III Corps was divided, with one division at White Oak Swamp, and the other at Bottom's Bridge. Neither division was close enough to offer Keyes immediate assistance if he was attacked. In effect, McClellan had shuffled his politically unreliable commanders off to the south, where it was expected they would see no action, and win no laurels. Their under-strength divisions were out on a limb, and while McClellan considered it unlikely that the defensive-minded Johnston would attack, the officers and men of Keyes' III Corps were well aware of how exposed their position was.

On 30 May 1862, General Johnston informed Davis and Lee that he planned to attack the enemy the following day. Beyond that, he kept the details of his dispositions and attack plans to himself, informing his subordinates on a "need to know" basis. He was well aware of Union dispositions, and saw the deployment of Keyes' IV Corps at Seven Pines as virtually an invitation to attack it. Seven Pines lay at a crossroads where the Williamsburg Road and the Nine Mile Road met. Both roads led towards Richmond and the Confederate army. To the south, the Charles City Road slipped past the flank of the Union position, and roads also linked it to the crossroads. The three Union Corps to the north of the Chickahominy would have to cross the river using makeshift bridges, which made any such redeployment slow, if not impossible. If he could strike Keyes and Heintzelman before they could be reinforced, he would deal McClellan a crushing blow. Even a defensive-minded general could appreciate a golden offensive opportunity when it was presented to him.

One great advantage of McClellan's Army of the Potomac over its Confederate opponents was the considerable logistical tail available to the Union troops. This photograph of a Union encampment near the White House terminus of the Richmond and York River Railroad helps suggest the scale of the logistical enterprise. (Stratford Archive)

His plan was relatively simple. Johnston divided his army into three "wings" (the formal arrangement of his army into Corps lay in the future). The divisions of D.R. Jones and Lafayette McLaws formed the army "Reserve", under John B. Magruder, charged with screening the enemy across the Chickahominy. Gustavus Smith's "Left Wing" consisted of his own division (temporarily commanded by W.H.C. Whiting) and the division of A.P. Hill. Johnston had little faith in the abilities of his deputy, but he expected Whiting's Division to move east down the Nine Mile Road in support of Longstreet's attack. James Longstreet, commanding the "Right Wing", was going to spearhead the two-pronged attack. He retained control of his own division, which was expected to march down the Nine Mile Road to hit Keyes in the right flank. Longstreet also commanded D.H. Hill's Division, which was ordered to advance up the Williamsburg Road to hit Keyes in his front. Rodes' Brigade of D.H. Hill's Division was detached from the rest of the force, guarding the Charles City Road. Johnston ordered Huger's small division to march through Richmond to the Charles City Road and put pressure on the Union left flank. This would release Rodes, who could then rejoin D.H. Hill before the attack was launched. Huger's Division, along with Brigadier General J.E.B. Stuart's cavalry and the army artillery reserve, were not allocated to army "wings", but were kept under the direct control of Johnston. The trouble with this plan was that it relied on everything working smoothly. Johnston's inexperienced troops had to move into position during the night, and then his commanders had to launch a concerted attack while out of communication with each other. He also had to rely on his two principal commanders, Smith and Longstreet. Lately Smith suffered anxiety attacks during moments of crisis, which rendered him completely ineffective as a commander. For his part, Longstreet was considered dependable, but at Williamsburg appeared to lose control of the battle. Johnston gave his orders, and hoped everything would work according to plan.

OPPOSING COMMANDERS

UNION

Major General George Brinton McClellan (1826–85)

A son of Philadelphia, McClellan graduated from West Point in 1846, and was duly commissioned as a lieutenant in the engineers. He served with distinction during the Mexican–American War, winning two brevet promotions, and emerged from the war with the brevet rank of colonel. In the spring of 1855, he formed part of a delegation sent to Europe to observe European armies in action during the Crimean War (1854–56). He witnessed the siege of Sevastopol, and on his return he published his report, entitled *The Armies of Europe*. He resigned his commission in 1857 to become the chief engineer on the Illinois State Railroad, and within three years had become the President of the Ohio & Mississippi Railroad Company. When the war began McClellan was living in Ohio, and consequently he was offered and accepted a commission as major general of the Ohio volunteers. His performance in western Virginia (now West Virginia) earned him a commission as major general in the regular army, and brought him to the attention of his superiors in Washington. President Lincoln named him commander of the Washington defenses, and gave him command of the fledgling Army of the Potomac, which had just been defeated at Manassas (July 1861). McClellan had a flair for military administration and through his efforts the army was transformed from a defeated force into a well-trained and superbly equipped army, capable of resuming the offensive against the Confederates.

He proved a popular commander, and both the army and the nation had great confidence in McClellan, who was nicknamed "Little Napoleon" by the press. Unfortunately his administrative genius was not matched by his military abilities.

During the Peninsula Campaign McClellan proved an overcautious commander, and continually requested more men, despite heavily outnumbering his Confederate opponents. His caution led to delay outside Yorktown while he prepared a formal siege, and his hesitation before Richmond allowed first Johnston and later Lee to seize the initiative. After the debacle of the Seven Days Battles he retained his command but lost the confidence of his men and his president. After further lackluster performances during the Second Manassas and Antietam (Sharpsburg) campaigns, McClellan was removed from his command.

Brigadier General Edwin Vose Sumner (1797–1863)

A native of Boston, Sumner entered the army as a second lieutenant of cavalry in 1819, and served in both garrison duties and on the western frontier, and by 1838 he commanded the army's cavalry school. During the Mexican-American War, Major Sumner commanded the 2nd US

Brigadier General Edwin V. Sumner commanded the Army of the Potomac's II Corps during the Peninsula Campaign. His rapid reinforcement of the Union positions south of the Chickahominy River during the battle of Fair Oaks helped prevent the collapse of the Union left wing. (Stratford Archive)

Brigadier General Samuel P. Heintzelman with his III Corps of the Army of the Potomac was posted to the south and east of the IV Corps positions around Fair Oaks and Seven Pines. He was forced to redeploy his troops to meet the Confederate attack on 31 May. (Library of Congress)

Dragoon Regiment, and led a charge at Medelin near Vera Cruz that broke a regiment of Mexican lancers. He was badly wounded at the battle of Cerro Gordo while leading the mounted rifle regiment, but his gallantry ensured his brevet promotion to lieutenant colonel. He went on to command the army's cavalry at the battle of Molina del Rey. After the conflict he became the military Governor of the New Mexico Territory before being sent on a fact-finding mission to Europe to study European cavalry tactics. He returned to take up the post of Military Governor in Kansas, and in 1858, was named the commander of the Department of the West. When the Civil War began Sumner was in California and requested an appointment in the Eastern Theater. He assisted General McClellan in his reorganization of the Army of the Potomac, then in May 1862, took command of the army's II Corps.

During the battle of Fair Oaks his reinforcement of the Union front line avoided a catastrophe, and Sumner was largely responsible for re-organizing the army after the first day's fighting, a task that should have been undertaken by McClellan himself.

He commanded II Corps during the Seven Days and Second Manassas campaigns, then continued to hold senior command in the Army of the Potomac until his death from congestion of the lungs in March 1863.

Brigadier General Samuel Peter Heintzelman (1805–80)

Born into the German community of Lancaster County, Pennsylvania, Heintzelman went to West Point, graduating in 1826, at which point he was commissioned as a second lieutenant in the infantry. For two decades he served on the western frontier and in Florida, where he participated in the fighting against the Seminoles. During the Mexican–American War he was decorated for gallantry, and in October 1847 Heintzelman was made a brevet major. After the war he served in California, and fought against the Coyote and Yuma tribes along the Colorado River during his six-year tour on the West Coast. In 1859–60 he was posted to Texas, where he led patrols along the Rio Grande as a deterrent against Mexican marauders. When the Civil War began he was promoted to lieutenant colonel and sent to Washington D.C., where he briefly held an administrative post before being selected as the colonel of the 17th US Infantry. By late May 1861, he was promoted to a brigadier general of volunteers, and two months later he commanded a division during the Bull Run campaign. When General McClellan reorganized the Army of the Potomac in March 1862, Heintzelman was appointed to command the army's III Corps, a post he held during the Peninsula Campaign.

This veteran soldier fought well during the battle of Williamsburg and at Fair Oaks, commanding most of IV Corps as well as his own during the Fair Oaks fight. He was duly promoted to brevet brigadier general in the regular army for his services. After the campaign he continued to command III Corps during the Second Manassas campaign. During the Antietam campaign his III Corps remained in the Washington defenses. On 12 October 1862, he was relieved of Corps command and assigned to the Military District of Washington, remaining in the capital for almost two years. He ended the war in command of the Northern Department headquartered at Columbus, Ohio.

Brigadier General Erasmus Darwin Keyes (1810–95)

The son of a Massachusetts surgeon, Keyes selected the army rather than medicine as a career, and graduated from West Point in 1832. He was commissioned as a lieutenant in the 3rd Artillery Regiment, and after serving in the Southern states during the nullification troubles of 1832–33, he was appointed to the staff of General Winfield Scott. Promoted to the rank of captain in 1837, he spent the next decade advising Scott on the military situation on the western frontier. From 1854 to 1858 he taught artillery tactics at West Point, then rejoined General Scott's staff as military secretary to the commander of the army. Promoted to the rank of colonel shortly after the Civil War began, he was duly promoted to a brigadier general of volunteers in June 1861. He commanded the first brigade of the 1st Division with distinction during the Manassas campaign of 1861. President Lincoln named him the commander of the Army of the Potomac's IV Corps in March 1862, and he held the command throughout the Peninsula Campaign. When McClellan withdrew his army from the Peninsula, Keyes remained behind to defend the Union foothold around Yorktown and Fort Monroe.

His performed reasonably well during the campaign, and was subsequently confirmed as a brigadier general of the regular army as a result of his actions. He went on to hold minor appointments until he resigned from the army in 1864, then moved to California where he became a successful businessman.

Brigadier General Erasmus D. Keyes commanded the IV Corps of McClellan's army. His troops bore the full brunt of the Confederate attack at Fair Oaks. (Stratford Archive)

CONFEDERATE

General Joseph Eggleston Johnston (1807–91)

Johnston graduated from West Point in 1829 alongside fellow Virginian Robert E. Lee. He was commissioned into the artillery, but resigned his commission in 1837 after eight years of service to take up a more lucrative post as a civil engineer. Civilian life proved less than ideal, and Johnston returned to the army in 1838, when he was commissioned as a first lieutenant in the Corps of Engineers. A skilled topographical engineer, he saw service in the Seminole Wars and received a brevet promotion to captain before distinguishing himself during the Mexican–American War. He was wounded at the battle of Cerro Gordo and again at Chapultepec, but was rewarded for his actions by the award of two brevet promotions, and he ended the war as a brevet lieutenant colonel. He held a variety of posts over the following decade before being appointed as the army's quartermaster general in June 1860, when he was also promoted to the rank of brigadier general. Johnston resigned his commission in April 1861 following the secession of Virginia from the Union, and he was immediately made a major general of the Virginia volunteers. The following month he was commissioned as a brigadier general of the regular Confederate army, and in June he was given command of the Army of the Shenandoah. His superb performance during the Manassas campaign of July 1861 won him command of the Confederate Army of the Potomac and promotion to general. He was also given command of the military Department of Northern Virginia, and held both posts until he was wounded at the battle of Fair Oaks on 31 May 1862.

General Joseph E. Johnston was known as a skilled defensive general, but he was reluctant to confront McClellan unless he had something akin to parity of numbers. This said, at Fair Oaks he saw the chance to defeat the enemy in detail, and seized the opportunity. (National Archives)

Major General James Longstreet was a competent battlefield commander, but like his superior Johnston, he was poor at operational planning. Mistakes made by him during the advance to Fair Oaks helped rob the Confederates of a decisive victory. (Valentine Museum, Richmond, VA.)

Major General Gustavus W. Smith was psychologically unsuited for high command, as he was prone to withdrawal and inactivity in times of crisis. He contributed little to the Confederate cause at Fair Oaks. (Valentine Museum, Richmond, VA.)

Although a gifted commander, Johnston never enjoyed the full confidence of President Davis. He proved more than a match for General McClellan during the Peninsula Campaign, and his counterattack at Fair Oaks effectively halted the Union advance and saved Richmond. Although he developed a reputation for retreating, he was recognized by both friend and foe as one of the most able commanders of the war. After the Peninsula Campaign he commanded the Army of the Tennessee (1863–64).

Major General James Longstreet (1821–1904)

The quiet South Carolinian graduated near the bottom of his class in West Point (1842), but distinguished himself during the Mexican–American War, and ended the war as a brevet major. He had to wait until 1858 before he was officially promoted to major, and served as paymaster until he resigned his commission in June 1861. Commissioned as a brigadier general, he saw service at First Manassas (21 July 1861), and was promoted to major general on 7 October. Although officially he commanded a division during the Fair Oaks campaign, in effect he was elevated to command a Corps-sized wing of the Confederate Army during the latter stages of the campaign. After the campaign he was appointed a lieutenant general, and his position as a corps commander was confirmed. He served as Robert E. Lee's principal lieutenant until the final surrender at Appomattox in April 1865.

A religious man, his once jovial character was crushed by the death of his two children in 1862, and from that point on he appeared withdrawn, taciturn and aloof. His military skills were highly developed, and despite occasional blunders such as his failure to communicate his orders clearly before the Fair Oaks battle, his comrades and enemies rated him as one of the most skilled Corps commanders of the war.

Major General Gustavus Woodson Smith (1821–96)

This Kentucky-born engineer graduated 8th out of his class of 56 at West Point in 1842, and served in the Mexican–American War. Subsequently he became an Assistant Professor of Engineering at his old college, and contributed to the design of sea-coast fortifications until his resignation from the army in 1854. While pursuing a civilian career as a civil engineer, Smith dabbled in politics, becoming New York's streets commissioner in 1858. On 19 September 1861, he accepted a commission as a major general in the Confederate army, and despite his ill health he was given a field command in Virginia.

During the Peninsula Campaign he served ostensibly as a divisional commander, but his senior rank and largely undeserved reputation ensured his selection for higher command. During the battle of Fair Oaks he commanded a Corps-sized force, and as senior officer in the field he assumed command of the army late on 31 March when General Johnston was wounded. Unable to cope with the physical and mental pressures of army command, he was replaced by Robert E. Lee.

Major General John Bankhead Magruder (1807–71)

"Prince John" was born in Winchester, Virginia, and elected to follow a career in the army. He graduated from West Point in 1830, whereupon he was commissioned as a second lieutenant in the 7th US Infantry. He trans-

Brigadier General James E.B. Stuart did not play a major role in the battle, but his subsequent ride around McClellan's army did much to raise Confederate spirits in the weeks that followed. The operation also provided General R.E. Lee with the information he needed to plan the Seven Days campaign. This sketch shows Stuart (standing, right) surrounded by his staff. (Valentine Museum, Richmond)

ferred to the artillery arm, and after a spell at the artillery school at Fort Monroe he was formally appointed to the 1st US Artillery in August 1861. He went on to serve in a variety of coastal fortifications on the Atlantic seaboard, and participated in the Seminole War in Florida (1837–38) before being sent to Texas in 1845. During the Mexican–American War he served as a captain of artillery at the Siege of Vera Cruz, and at the battles of Palo Alto and Resaca de la Palma (1846). He was breveted a major after distinguishing himself at the battle of Cerro Gordo (1847), and ended the war as a brevet colonel. For the next decade he served in various coastal fortifications and frontier posts until he resigned his commission to join the Confederate army when Virginia seceded.

An encampment of Union troops. During the months before the Peninsula Campaign, the Army of the Potomac drilled, practiced tactics, and prepared itself for the coming campaign. This scene depicts the encampment of the 61st New York, a regiment in the 1st Division of General Sumner's II Corps. (Stratford Archive)

Magruder was nicknamed "Prince John" because of his flamboyant social life and his elegant appearance, and was described as "the wittiest man in the old army." This colorful persona was matched by an aptitude for soldiering. The Confederate government recognized his potential, and promoted him to brigadier general. While commanding the Confederate forces around Yorktown he successfully duped General McClellan as to his strength, and bought precious time, a deception that probably saved Richmond and the Confederacy. During the Seven Days Battles his lack of aggression led to his removal from command, and Magruder was reassigned to Texas, where he took command of the defenses of the Confederate far west.

Brigadier General James Ewell Brown Stuart (1833–64)

Born in Patrick County, Virginia, J.E.B. Stuart graduated 13th in his class at West Point in 1854, and was assigned to the cavalry. When Virginia seceded from the Union in 1861 he resigned his commission and became the colonel of the 1st Virginia Cavalry. His performance during the Manassas campaign of July 1861 caught the attention of both his superiors and the imagination of the public. Consequently he was promoted to the rank of brigadier general on 24 September, and given command of the army's fledgling cavalry arm. During the Peninsula Campaign he performed his duties with great *elan*, and his circumnavigation of the Army of the Potomac became one of the great feats of the war.

Stuart was known for his dashing appearance, wearing a black plume in his hat and a well-cut uniform on campaign. He also expected that his officers follow his example, a calculated move to emphasize the elite nature of his Virginia cavalry, and one of the tools he used to establish his superiority over his opponents. Later in the war J.E.B. Stuart was openly criticized for operational blunders, and it is probable that he was less suited to command a full cavalry corps than a division. This said, during the Peninsula Campaign the performance of Stuart and his Confederate horsemen exceeded all expectations.

OPPOSING ARMIES

THE UNION ARMY

With some justification, George B. McClellan considered the Army of the Potomac to be his own creation. It was certainly no longer the army that had been defeated at Manassas. Since his arrival in Washington in late July 1861, McClellan had worked hard to improve the army's morale, and to ensure it was equipped with the very best arms and equipment. His first action was to call for a fresh army of almost 300,000 men and, although Lincoln rejected this request, McClellan managed to recruit an army of some 200,000 men; more than double the force available to Johnston. What followed was a lengthy period of training, morale building and the enforcement of army discipline on what was essentially a citizen militia. To a large extent, the responsibility for training these raw troops fell to Brigadier General Casey, the man who would bear the brunt of the initial Confederate attack at Fair Oaks. His division was used as a training formation, and once his men were deemed of a sufficient standard, they were allocated to other commanders, and Casey was given fresh troops to work with. It was his singular misfortune that when his division embarked for the Peninsula, he had insufficient time to train his new batch of troops to his exacting standard. Nevertheless, during the winter of 1861–62, the troops learned to march, to drill and, at least in theory, to fight. Regular regiments from the old army provided a steady example for the commanders of these volunteer formations to emulate, and slowly the Army of the Potomac was transformed into a potent force; the largest, best armed and the most lavishly equipped military force yet assembled on the American continent.

McClellan later saw the creation of the Army of the Potomac as his greatest achievement. He regarded "*the creation of such an army in so short a time from nothing will hereafter be regarded as one of the highest glories of the administration and the nation.*" The French military observer the Prince of Joinville went even further. He wrote: "*Never, we believe, has any nation created, of herself, by her own will, by her single resources, without coercion of any kind, without government pressure, and in such a short space of time, so considerable an armament.*" While the soldiers themselves appreciated that "Little Mac" was furnishing them with the training and equipment they needed, the politicians and newspapermen saw things differently. To them the army was a wasted resource; a vast, expensive personal bodyguard for McClellan rather than an offensive force that could end the war in a single campaign. This was McClellan's real stratagem; to create an army that was unstoppable, and which could achieve victory through overwhelming the opposition, thereby keeping bloodshed and economic damage to a minimum.

Brigadier General Silas Casey was the main drill expert in the Army of the Potomac, and he supervised the training of most of the army's recruits during the six months before the campaign began. He also commanded the division deployed around Seven Pines that was attacked on 31 May 1862. (National Archives)

A Union 13in. Seacoast Mortar, one of the most powerful pieces of ordnance in the Union arsenal. The Confederates were unable to match the size and effectiveness of the Union artillery train. (Library of Congress)

When McClellan was demoted from Commander in Chief of the Union army to command simply of the Army of the Potomac, Secretary of War Edwin Stanton took over control of the war. When McClellan left for the Peninsula, Stanton almost immediately took McDowell's I Corps from the Army of the Potomac, and over the coming weeks the return of this missing Corps dominated McClellan's strategic planning, and provided a ready excuse for his failure to defeat the enemy. Even without it, "Little Mac" had the troops he needed for the job. He launched his campaign with the III and IV Corps at his disposal, and within a week Sumner's II Corps had joined the army in front of Yorktown. In addition he had a powerful reserve artillery group, a small cavalry wing and a logistical train that would have been the envy of any commander. To McClellan, it was still not enough. The dispatch of reinforcements allowed him to increase the size of his army, stripping some of his existing corps and amalgamating these with reinforcements to form two new Army Corps (V and VI Corps). By the time of the battle of Fair Oaks, all his Corps consisted of two divisions, each of two or three brigades and an artillery contingent. According to his reports to Washington, in late May his army consisted of 89,000 combat troops. In fact, using the same counting scheme he applied to the Confederates, he had 103,382 troops at his disposal and ready for duty. In addition losses were caused by sickness, the deployment of garrisons to guard his supply lines and of course the detachment of McDowell's force. The 155,000 men he had in Washington had been cut by a third when Johnston fell upon the Army of the Potomac at Fair Oaks.

Morale within the army was relatively high, and everyone had high expectations. The Army of the Potomac had the men, supplies and equipment to defeat the Confederates, and the soldiers had trained long and hard for their chance to bring the enemy to battle. Despite the delays encountered outside Yorktown, the average soldier was keen to drive on to Richmond and end the war in a single climactic engagement. The failure to achieve this led to the sapping of army resolve, but only after the Fair Oaks fight. Even more importantly, it led to a lack of confidence in McClellan, inviting a strategic paralysis that allowed Lee to seize the initiative on the Peninsula.

ORDER OF BATTLE,
The Army of the Potomac, Fair Oaks, 31 May 1862

Army of the Potomac –
MajGen George B. McClellan

Headquarters Guard:
2nd US Cavalry
4th US Cavalry (2 Coys.)
McClellan Dragoons (Illinois)
Oneida Cavalry (New York)
Sturgis Rifles (Illinois)
93rd New York (4 Coys.)
8th US Infantry (2 Coys.)

II Corps – BrigGen Edwin V. Sumner

1st Division – BrigGen Israel B. Richardson
Attached: Co. D, 6th New York Cavalry

1st Brigade – BrigGen Oliver O. Howard
5th New Hampshire
61st New York
64th New York
81st Pennsylvania

2nd Brigade – BrigGen Thomas F. Meagher
63rd New York
69th New York
88th New York

3rd Brigade – BrigGen William H. French
52nd New York
57th New York
66th New York
53rd Pennsylvania

Divisional Artillery – Capt George W. Hazzard
2 Btys., 1st New York Light Arty. (Btys. B & G)
3 Btys., 4th US Arty. (Btys. A–C)

2nd Division – BrigGen John Sedgwick
Attached: Co. K, 6th New York Cavalry

1st Brigade – BrigGen Willis A. Gorman
15th Massachusetts (1st Co., Minnesota Sharpshooters attached)
1st Minnesota (2nd Co., Minnesota Sharpshooters attached)
34th New York
82nd New York

2nd Brigade – BrigGen William W. Burns
69th Pennsylvania
71st Pennsylvania
72nd Pennsylvania
106th Pennsylvania

3rd Brigade – BrigGen N.J.T. Dana
19th Massachusetts
20th Massachusetts
7th Michigan
42nd New York

Divisional Artillery – Col C.H. Tomkins
3 Btys., 1st Rhode Island Light Arty. (Btys. A, B & G)
Bty I, 1st US Arty.

III Corps – BrigGen Samuel P. Heintzelman

Attached: 3rd Pennsylvania Cavalry – Col William W. Averell

2nd Division – BrigGen Joseph Hooker
1st Brigade – BrigGen Cuvier Grover

2nd New Hampshire
1st Massachusetts
11th Massachusetts
26th Pennsylvania

2nd Brigade – BrigGen Daniel E. Sickles
70th New York
71st New York
72nd New York
73rd New York
74th New York

3rd Brigade – BrigGen Francis E. Patterson
5th New Jersey
6th New Jersey
7th New Jersey
8th New Jersey

Divisional Artillery – Maj Charles S. Wainwright
Bty. D, 1st New York Light Arty.
Bty. H, 1st US Arty.
6th New York Independent Light Bty.
4th New York Independent Light Bty.

3rd Division BrigGen Philip Kearny

1st Brigade – BrigGen Charles D. Jameson
87th New York
57th Pennsylvania
63rd Pennsylvania
105th Pennsylvania

2nd Brigade – BrigGen David B. Birney
3rd Maine
4th Maine
38th New York
40th New York

3rd Brigade – BrigGen Hiram G. Berry
2nd Michigan
3rd Michigan
5th Michigan
37th New York

Divisional Artillery – Capt James Thomson
Bty. B, 1st New Jersey Light Arty.
Bty. E, 1st Rhode Island Light Arty.
Bty. G, 2nd US Arty.
6th New York Independent Light Bty.
4th New York Independent Light Bty.

IV Corps – BrigGen Erasmus D. Keyes

Attached: 8th Pennsylvania Cavalry – Col David McM. Gregg

1st Division – BrigGen Darius N. Couch
Attached: Co. F, 6th New York Cavalry

1st Brigade – BrigGen John J. Peck
55th New York
62nd New York
93rd New York
102nd Pennsylvania

2nd Brigade – BrigGen John J. Abercrombie
65th New York
67th New York
23rd Pennsylvania
31st Pennsylvania
61st Pennsylvania

3rd Brigade – BrigGen Charles Devens
2nd Massachusetts
10th Massachusetts
36th New York

Divisional Artillery – Maj Robert M. West
4 Btys., 1st Pennsylvania Light Arty. (Btys. C, D, E & H)

2nd Division – BrigGen Silas Casey
Attached: Co. H, 6th New York Cavalry

1st Brigade – BrigGen Henry M. Naglee
11th Maine
56th New York
100th New York
53rd Pennsylvania
104th Pennsylvania

2nd Brigade – BrigGen Henry W. Wessells
96th New York
85th Pennsylvania
101st Pennsylvania
103rd Pennsylvania

3rd Brigade – BrigGen Innis N. Palmer
81st New York
85th New York
92nd New York
98th New York

Divisional Artillery – Col Guilford D. Bailey
2 Btys., 1st New York Light Arty. (Btys. A&H)
7th New York Independent Light Bty.
8th New York Independent Light Bty.

V Corps – BrigGen Fitz John Porter

1st Division – BrigGen George W. Morell
Attached: 1st US Sharpshooters – Col Hiram Berdan

1st Brigade – BrigGen John H. Martindale
2nd Maine
18th Massachusetts
13th New York
25th New York

2nd Brigade – BrigGen James McQuade
9th Massachusetts
4th Michigan
14th New York
83rd Pennsylvania

3rd Brigade – BrigGen Daniel Butterfield
16th Michigan (company of Michigan Sharpshooters attached)
12th New York
17th New York
44th New York
83rd Pennsylvania

Divisional Artillery – Capt Charles Griffin
2 Btys., 1st Massachusetts Light Arty. (Btys. C&E)
Bty. C, 1st Rhode Island Light Arty.
Bty. D, 5th US Arty.

2nd Division – BrigGen George Sykes

1st Brigade – Col Robert C Buchanan
3rd US Infantry
4th US Infantry
12th US Infantry
14th US Infantry

2nd Brigade – LtCol William Chapman
2nd US Infantry
6th US Infantry
10th US Infantry
11th US Infantry
17th US Infantry

3rd Brigade – Col Gouverneur K. Warren
5th New York
1st Connecticut Heavy Artillery (infantry)

VI Corps – BrigGen William B. Franklin

Attached: 1st New York Cavalry – Col David McM. Gregg

1st Division – BrigGen Henry W. Slocum

1st Brigade – BrigGen W. Taylor
1st New Jersey
2nd New Jersey
3rd New Jersey
4th New Jersey

2nd Brigade – Col Joseph J. Bartlett
5th Maine
16th New York
27th New York
96th Pennsylvania

3rd Brigade – BrigGen John Newton
18th New York
31st New York
32nd New York
95th Pennsylvania

Divisional Artillery – Capt Edward R. Platt
Bty. A, 1st Massachusetts Light Arty.
Bty. A, 1st New Jersey Light Arty.
Bty. D, 2nd US Arty.

2nd Division – BrigGen William F. Smith
Attached: Coys D & E, 5th Pennsylvania Cavalry

1st Brigade – BrigGen Winfield S. Hancock
6th Maine
43rd New York
49th Pennsylvania
5th Wisconsin

2nd Brigade – BrigGen W.T.H. Brooks
2nd Vermont
3rd Vermont
4th Vermont
5th Vermont
6th Vermont

3rd Brigade – BrigGen John W. Davidson
7th Maine
33rd New York
49th New York
77th New York

Divisional Artillery – Capt Romeyn B. Ayres
Bty. E, 1st New York Light Arty.
1st New York Independent Light Arty. Bty.
3rd New York Independent Light Arty. Bty.
Bty. F, 5th US Arty.

Army Assets

Artillery Reserve – Col Henry J. Hunt

1st Brigade – LtCol William Hays
Bty. M, 2nd US Arty.
5 Btys., 3rd US Arty. (Btys. C–G)

2nd Brigade – LtCol George W. Getty
6 Btys., E, 1st US Arty. (Btys. C & G–K)
Bty. G, 4th US Arty.
2 Btys., 5th US Arty. (Btys. A & K)

3rd Brigade – Maj Albert Arndt
4 Btys., 1st New York Arty. Btn. (Btys. A–D)

4th Brigade – Capt J. Howard Carlisle
Bty. E, 2nd US Arty.
6 Btys., 3rd US Arty. (Btys. F-K)

Cavalry Reserve – BrigGen Philip St George Cooke

1st Brigade – BrigGen William H. Emory
6th Pennsylvania Cavalry
5th US Cavalry
6th US Cavalry

2nd Brigade – BrigGen George A.H. Blake
8th Pennsylvania
1st US Cavalry

Army Engineers – BrigGen Daniel P. Woodbury
15th New York Engineers
50th New York Engineers
3 Coys., US Engineer Bn. – Capt James C. Duane

Advanced Guard – BrigGen George Stoneman
2nd Rhode Island
98th Pennsylvania
8th Illinois Cavalry
12 Btys., 2nd US Arty. (Btys. A–L)

Independent Command – LtCol Rufus Ingalls
93rd New York (6 Coys.)
11th Pennsylvania Cavalry (5 Coys.)
Bty. F, 1st New York Light Arty.

THE CONFEDERATE ARMY

There was no single Confederate army in Virginia. A somewhat confusing and decentralized command system meant that General Magruder in Yorktown, General Huger in Norfolk and General Johnston in Fredericksburg had no authority outside their own encampments. President Jefferson Davis and his Secretary of War Judah P. Benjamin held the strategic reins, leaving no single commander in charge in the Virginia theater. Also, relations between Davis and Johnston were becoming increasingly strained. The rift had begun the previous summer. Johnston felt himself slighted by the President's ranking of senior Confederate generals, placing him fourth on the list instead of first. This meant he was outranked by his former West Point classmate Robert E. Lee, although the latter's authority was limited as he held a staff rather than a field command. In the spring of 1862, Robert E. Lee was *"assigned to duty at the seat of government … under the direction of the President."* Although he was officially little more than the senior military advisor to the President, Davis respected Lee's judgment, and allowed him to issue orders on his behalf. This made him the de facto Commanding General of the Confederate army. This said, Lee was always punctilious in consulting the President, and the two maintained a reasonably harmonious relationship. Consequently, Davis usually trusted Lee to make decisions on his behalf, and to supervise the larger picture, at least in the Eastern Theater. Lee made crucial decisions during the course of the campaign, the most important being the deployment of General "Stonewall" Jackson to the Shenandoah Valley, charged with tying down Union forces there. He actually managed to pin over 100,000 Union troops in Washington, the Shenandoah and northern Virginia. Equally important was the reinforcement of Johnston's army with troops from the Carolinas, the abandonment of Norfolk that provided Johnston with the additional troops of Huger's command, and the improvement of the James River defenses at Drewry's Bluff, which protected Richmond from naval attack.

No official Corps structure existed in Johnston's army. At the time of the withdrawal from Yorktown, the army was divided into four "wings", under Longstreet, D.H. Hill, Smith, and Magruder. Longstreet, Smith and Hill's commands were little more than oversized divisions, but Magruder commanded the division of McLaws and the small division of D.R. Jones. Johnston retained direct control of the cavalry, the artillery reserve, and two brigade-sized garrisons stationed at Williamsburg and Jamestown. Three days before the battle of Fair Oaks, on 28

The French military observer the Prince de Joinville (seated, fourth from left) was one of several foreign officers who accompanied the Army of the Potomac during the campaign. Many saw it as the most significant military enterprise of the war so far, and were eager to see how the army performed. (Stratford Archive)

May, Johnston reorganized his army into three "wings", under Longstreet, Smith and Magruder. The latter composed the "left wing" (later designated the reserve), and consisted of the same two divisions (McClaws' and D.R. Jones') and the six brigades that Magruder had commanded at Yorktown. D.H. Hill's division of five brigades was placed under Longstreet's command, who also retained his own oversized six-brigade division, forming the "right wing". Smith controlled the "center" (later designated the left wing), comprising his own division of five brigades (temporarily commanded by Whiting), and the four-brigade division of A.P. Hill. As before, Johnston retained control of Stuart's cavalry, Pendleton's artillery reserve, garrison troops, and the three-brigade division of Huger, which was transferred to Johnston's command the day before he launched his attack, adding another 7,400 men to the army. With the newly organized division of A.P. Hill

A Union skirmish line. Although proficient in drill and weapons handling, the bulk of the army was still inexperienced, and their performance during the opening skirmishes of the campaign was erratic. These troops were sketched in action during the attack on Dam No. 1 on the Warwick River, on 16 April 1862. (Stratford Archive)

(consisting of approximately 10,000 men), Johnston had a total of 94,813 men under his direct command, giving him something akin to parity of numbers with the Army of the Potomac. This number is higher than Johnston's own total of 72,239 men, as the lower tally represented "duty strength", omitting men with noncombatant roles such as troops bringing up supplies, in hospital or in administrative posts.

Morale in the army was reasonably high, but although some regiments had already endured their baptism of fire at Manassas and Ball's Bluff, others had yet to experience the realities of war at first hand. The divisions of R.H. Anderson and D.H. Hill in Longstreet's command were considered veteran troops, as were the troopers of Stuart's cavalry and most of the gunners of Pendleton's artillery reserve. Lee had worked hard to ensure that Johnston received the supplies and munitions he needed to launch a counterattack against the Union invaders, and for once the Confederates had local superiority in numbers. In the end it was not the ability of the troops that turned opportunity into bloody stalemate, but the shortcomings of the Confederate commanders.

ORDER OF BATTLE,
Confederate Army in Virginia, Fair Oaks, 31 May 1862

Confederate Army in Virginia – General Joseph E. Johnston

Left Wing – MajGen Gustavus W. Smith

BrigGen William H.C. Whiting's Division (formerly G.W. Smith's Division)

Col Evander McIver Law's Brigade (formerly Whiting's Brigade)
4th Alabama
2nd Mississippi
11th Mississippi
6th North Carolina
Balthis' Bty. (Virginia)
Reilly's Bty. (North Carolina)

BrigGen James J. Pettigrew's Brigade
1st Arkansas (battalion)
35th Georgia
2nd North Carolina
47th Virginia
Andrews' 1st Maryland Bty.

BrigGen Wade Hampton's Brigade
14th Georgia
19th Georgia
16th North Carolina
Hampton's Legion (South Carolina)
Moody's Bty. (Louisiana)

BrigGen Robert Hatton's Brigade
1st Tennessee
7th Tennessee
14th Tennessee

BrigGen John B. Hood's Brigade
18th Georgia
1st Texas
4th Texas
5th Texas

MajGen A.P. Hill's Division

BrigGen Charles W. Field's Brigade
22nd Virginia (battalion)
40th Virginia
55th Virginia
Pegram's Bty. (Virginia)

BrigGen Maxcy Gregg's Brigade
1st South Carolina

12th South Carolina
13th South Carolina
14th South Carolina
1st South Carolina Rifles
Davidson's Bty. (Virginia)

BrigGen Joseph R. Anderson's Brigade
45th Georgia
49th Georgia
3rd Louisiana (battalion)
34th North Carolina
38th North Carolina
McIntosh's Bty. (South Carolina)
Crenshaw's Bty. (Virginia)

BrigGen Lawrence O'B. Branch's Brigade
7th North Carolina
12th North Carolina
18th North Carolina
28th North Carolina
33rd North Carolina
37th North Carolina
Branch's Bty. (North Carolina)
Johnson's Bty. (Virginia)

Right Wing – MajGen James Longstreet

MajGen Daniel H. Hill's Division

BrigGen Samuel Garland Jr.'s Brigade
2nd Florida
2nd Mississippi (battalion)
5th North Carolina
23rd North Carolina
24th Virginia
38th Virginia
Bondurant's "Jeff Davis" Bty. (Alabama)

BrigGen Robert E. Rodes' Brigade
5th Alabama
6th Alabama
12th Alabama
12th Mississippi
4th Virginia Heavy Artillery (infantry)
Carter's Bty. (Virginia)

Col George B. Anderson's Brigade (formerly Featherstone's Brigade)
27th Georgia
28th Georgia
4th North Carolina
49th Virginia

BrigGen Gabriel J. Rains' Brigade
13th Alabama
26th Alabama
6th Georgia
23rd Georgia
Nelson's Bty. (Virginia)

BrigGen Henry A. Wise's Brigade (Temporarily attached to D.H. Hill's Division)
26th Virginia
47th Virginia
Armistead's Bty. (Virginia)
French's Bty. (Virginia)

Divisional Artillery
Hardaway's Bty. (Alabama)
Rhett's Bty. (South Carolina)

BrigGen Richard H. Anderson's Division (formerly Longstreet's Division)

Col Micah Jenkins' Brigade (formerly R.H. Anderson's Brigade)
4th South Carolina
5th South Carolina
6th South Carolina
Palmetto Sharpshooters (South Carolina)
1st Louisiana Zouaves (St Paul's Foot Rifles attached)
Stribling's Bty. (Virginia)

Col James L. Kemper's Brigade
1st Virginia
7th Virginia
11th Virginia
17th Virginia
Roger's Bty. (Virginia)

BrigGen George E. Pickett's Brigade
8th Virginia
18th Virginia
19th Virginia
28th Virginia
Dearing's Bty. (Virginia)

BrigGen Cadmus M. Wilcox's Brigade
9th Alabama
10th Alabama
11th Alabama
19th Mississippi
Stanard's (3rd) Coy., Richmond Howitzers

BrigGen Roger A. Pryor's Brigade
8th Alabama
14th Alabama
14th Louisiana
32nd Virginia
Macon's Bty. (Virginia)

BrigGen Raleigh E. Colston's Brigade
13th North Carolina
14th North Carolina
3rd Virginia

Divisional Artillery
Brown's (2nd) Coy., Richmond Howitzers
Maurin's Bty. (Louisiana)

BrigGen Benjamin Huger's Division

BrigGen Lewis A. Armistead's Brigade
5th Virginia (battalion)
9th Virginia
14th Virginia
53rd Virginia
Turner' Bty. (Virginia)

BrigGen W. Mahone's Brigade
3rd Alabama
12th Virginia
41st Virginia
Grimes' Bty. (Virginia)

BrigGen G.A. Blanchard's Brigade
3rd Georgia
4th Georgia
22nd Georgia
1st Louisiana
Huger's Bty. (Virginia)

Reserve – MajGen John B. Magruder

BrigGen Lafayette McLaws' Division

BrigGen Paul J. Semmes' Brigade

10th Georgia
5th Louisiana
10th Louisiana
15th Virginia
Noland's Battalion (Virginia)
Garrett's Bty. (Virginia)
Young's Bty. (Virginia)

BrigGen Richard Griffith's Brigade
13th Mississippi
18th Mississippi
21st Mississippi
McCarthy's (1st) Coy., Richmond Howitzers

BrigGen Joseph B. Kershaw's Brigade
2nd South Carolina
3rd South Carolina
7th South Carolina
8th South Carolina
Gracie's Battalion (Alabama)
Kemper's Bty. (Virginia)

BrigGen Howell Cobb's Brigade
16th Georgia
24th Georgia
2nd Louisiana
17th Mississippi
15th North Carolina
Cobb's Legion (Georgia)
Page's Bty. (Virginia)

BrigGen David R. Jones' Division

BrigGen Robert Toombs' Brigade
1st Georgia Regulars
2nd Georgia
15th Georgia
17th Georgia
20th Georgia
38th Georgia

BrigGen George T. Anderson's Brigade
7th Georgia
8th Georgia

9th Georgia
11th Georgia
1st Kentucky

Divisional Artillery – Col H.C. Cabell
Cosnahan's Bty. (Virginia)
Manly's Bty. (North Carolina)
Read's Bty. (Georgia)
Sand's Bty. (Virginia)

Army Assets

Artillery Reserve – BrigGen William N. Pendleton
Southall's Bty. (Virginia)
Carleton's Bty. (Georgia)
Richardson's Bty. (Virginia)
C.L. Smith's Bty. (Virginia)
Page's Bty. (Virginia)
Jordan's Bty. (Virginia)
Clarke's Bty. (Virginia)
Peyton's Bty. (Virginia)
Kirkpatrick's Bty. (Virginia)
4 Btys., Washington Artillery Bn. (Coys. 1–4) (Louisiana)
Chapman's "Dixie" Bty. (Virginia)

Cavalry Reserve – BrigGen J.E.B. Stuart
1st Virginia Cavalry
3rd Virginia Cavalry
4th Virginia Cavalry
9th Virginia Cavalry
Cobb's Legion Cavalry (Georgia)
Jeff Davis Legion Cavalry (Mississippi)
Hampton's Legion Cavalry (South Carolina)
Wise's Legion Cavalry (Virginia)
Stuart's Horse Arty. Bty.

THE CAMPAIGN

A Confederate sharpshooter during the Peninsula Campaign. Sharpshooters on both sides were kept busy during the Siege of Yorktown as they harassed enemy engineering operations, and provided a deterrent to active patrolling. (Stratford Archive)

On to Yorktown

On 17 March, the Army of the Potomac began boarding a fleet of transports anchored off Alexandria, and a series of convoys then steamed south, escorted by warships of the US Navy. On 1 April, McClellan himself embarked on the steamer *Commodore* and was taken south to Newport News, arriving off Fort Monroe the following day. He established his headquarters in the fort, where he discovered that Edwin Stanton had declared that General Wool and his 10,000 men were not under "Little Mac's" authority. For McClellan this was another indication of the pettiness of the Republican administration, as humiliating him came at the expense of weakening the Army of the Potomac.

Despite this setback, McClellan was determined to get the campaign under way immediately. General Wool informed him that the lower peninsula was defended by Major General John B. Magruder with approximately 12,000–15,000 men. McClellan regarded him as a *bon vivant* rather than a serious commander, and saw him as little threat. The previous summer the Confederates built a defensive line running in a south-westerly direction from the small port of Yorktown to the James River, some 12 miles away. The southern portion of this line was protected by the Warwick River, which flowed into the James. To improve the effectiveness of these defenses, Magruder built a series of five dams across this little river, flooding the marshy ground on its banks to create a more formidable barrier. Artillery emplacements were then built to cover the dams, which formed the only crossing points. From the headwaters of the Warwick River, Magruder's line stretched north through low-lying woodlands to Yorktown, where the old Revolutionary War defenses built by the British were strengthened and improved. In addition, gun positions were constructed to cover the York River, while a similar battery was constructed across the river at Gloucester Point.

During the early hours of 3 April, McClellan issued orders for an advance up the peninsula. He moved with uncharacteristic speed as he was keen to seize the initiative. He wrote to his wife: "*The grass will not grow under my feet*," and for once he was as good as his word. On 4 April, his army moved out, even though only two incomplete Corps were available for immediate use; those of Heintzelman (III Corps) and Keyes (IV Corps); a total of 66,700 men, including the army reserves.

On the right (or northern flank), Heintzelman advanced towards Yorktown, where he expected to encounter enemy entrenchments. On his left, and to the south, Keyes advanced towards the Warwick River, hoping to bypass the Confederate defenses around Yorktown and cut the defenders off from Richmond. Each Corps commander had two infantry divisions plus supporting artillery and cavalry at his disposal, while a fifth division followed on behind as McClellan's reserve. The day was pleasant,

1. The first Union troops come ashore at Fort Monroe in late March, and within a week two Corps are landed, along with their supplies. McClellan himself lands at Fort Monroe on 2 April. A third Corps (Sumner's II Corps) lands by 4 April.

2. On 4 April, III Corps (Heintzelman) and IV Corps (Keyes) advance on Magruder's forward positions around Big Bethel. Magruder's men fall back to their main line along the Warwick River.

3. Magruder had constructed a line of fortifications stretching from Yorktown in the north to the junction of the Warwick and James Rivers to the south. From 5 April on, this becomes a bulwark against the Union army.

4. The York River flank of Magruder's line is protected by a gun battery and troop emplacements at Gloucester Point, blocking passage up the York River to Union ships.

5. A large Confederate battery at Drewry's Bluff protects the James River approaches to Richmond, but the Confederates have only minor positions protecting the banks of the James River to the east of this point.

6. In April, Johnston rushed his army south to face McClellan at Yorktown. Longstreet commands the advanced guard, and assumes operational control over the Confederate forces in the lower Peninsula when he reaches Richmond. This effectively puts Magruder under Longstreet's command, bringing the entire Confederate force under the control of Johnston.

II SUMNER

③ ③

III HEINTZELMAN

IV KEYES

ARMY OF THE POTOMAC

Hampton

Fort Monroe

Hampton Roads

Mob Jack Bay

Gloucester

Gloucester Point

Yorktown

Warwick

Lee's Mill

Big Bethel

① ②

Halfway House

MAGRUDER

Rappahannock River

Urbanna

Piankatonk

York River

Williamsburg

James River

Surrey Courthouse

King & Queen's Courthouse

West Point

White House

New Kent Courthouse

Richmond & York River Railroad

King William Courthouse

Pamunkey River

Chickahominy River

Charles City Courthouse

Harrison's Landing

Blackwater

Norfolk & Petersburg Railroad

Hanover

Cold Harbour

Mechanicsville

Seven Pines ⑥

Hanover Junction

LONGSTREET

Malvern Hill

New Market

Bermuda Hundred

Drewry's Bluff ⑤

Virginia Central Railroad

Richmond & Danville RR

JOHNSTON

Richmond

Richmond & Petersburg Railroad

Petersburg

Weldon & Petersburg Railroad

Richmond, Fredericksburg & Potomac Railroad

20 miles

25 km

N

0

0

38

the enemy piquets withdrew as the Union troops advanced, and McClellan was filled with confidence. By nightfall the leading formations had covered over half the distance to their objectives, and McClellan wrote that: "*Everything has worked well today. I have gained some strong positions without fighting and shall try some more in manoeuvring tomorrow.*" He expected to begin the investment of Yorktown the following day, unaware that weather, terrain, and the enemy would conspire to sabotage his plans. While this was going on, Magruder was sending a stream of reports back to Richmond. President Davis and Robert E. Lee were now aware of McClellan's intent to attack Richmond from the east. A message was sent to General Johnston at Fredericksburg, ordering him to fall back to Richmond, then advance to support Magruder. This redeployment would clearly take time, and in the meantime, Magruder would have to delay the invaders as best he could. He was far from optimistic, writing: "*I have made my arrangements to fight with my small force, but without the slightest hope of success.*"

A "quaker" gun made from a tree trunk occupies an abandoned Confederate artillery position outside Manassas. The ability to deceive the enemy proved an important tool in the Confederate arsenal. (Library of Congress)

The roads of the Virginia Tidewater quickly turned to mud in heavy rain. In this engraving, showing an incident during the Union advance up the Peninsula from Hampton to Yorktown, a mule team pulling a supply wagon is shown stuck in the mud near Big Bethel in early April 1862. A Union soldier encourages the driver to continue. (Stratford Archive)

The following day (5 April) was a Sunday, and while McClellan and his staff attended a service, the Army of the Potomac resumed its advance. Although the two Union columns got under way soon after dawn, progress was slowed by a heavy downpour that lasted well into the afternoon. In his intelligence reports, McClellan had read that the roads in the Tidewater Peninsula were well drained. Nothing could have been further from the truth. The road surface in the region was composed of loam and shells, which quickly turned into a sludge. Beneath this, the soil was nothing but clay, and within hours the roads had turned into rivers of mud.

One Union officer later claimed that; "*such depth of mud and such frightful roads I never saw.*"

Rain and mud were not the only enemies. By mid-morning, Heintzelman sent McClellan a message informing him that the enemy were entrenched around Yorktown, with "*a large number of men …*" The Confederates opened fire as the Union columns approached, and the advance ground to a halt. To the south, Keyes reported encountering enemy positions along the Warwick River on the Lee's Mill Road, a place McClellan had expected to be undefended, or at least held with nothing more than a skirmish screen. A soldier from Maine recalled that as he "*emerged from a patch of woods we saw across the open space a long line of rebel earthworks with a stream in front,* [a] *rebel flag was flying and we could see the sesesh officers riding along the lines inside the works.*" Keyes added that he estimated an enemy column of up to 3,000 men was moving into position to block his advance, and that a frontal attack would be too costly. Also, Union intelligence had expected that the Warwick River would pose no real obstacle to the army's advance, but Magruder's damming and flooding had transformed the stream into an impassable obstacle. The second Union column also ground to a halt.

In fact very few Confederate troops occupied any part of Magruder's line. What the Union troops witnessed was the same handful of Confederate troops marching and counter-marching to give the appearance of greater numbers. One participant described what happened: "*This morning we were called out by the long wall and have been travelling most of the day, seeming with no other view than show ourselves to the enemy in as many different points of line as possible.*" Magruder was working

The headquarters of Brigadier General Heintzelman's III Corps in front of Yorktown was set up around Howe's Sawmill, some four miles east of the Confederate lines. Yorktown can be seen in the distance. (Stratford Archive)

hard at deceiving McClellan, making his handful of troops appear far more numerous than they actually were. Lieutenant Miller of the 14th Louisiana was even more descriptive: "*The way we fooled them was to divide each body of troops into two parts and keep them travelling all the time for twenty-four hours, until reinforcements came.*" His regiment made the journey from Yorktown to Lee's Mill six times that day. Captain McMath of the 11th Alabama described another trick. His regiment "*was ordered to cross open ground in plain sight of the enemy, until we got out of sight just around the point of the hill. We were halted there some half-hour when we were countermarched over to the place we started from.*"

Musicians and officers issued streams of signals and orders from the concealment of the woods, supply trains moved back and forth, and the exhausted Confederate troops continued to march and counter-march throughout the rest of the day, and into the next. Magruder was in his element, and in the words of a Southern diarist he; "*played his 10,000 before McClellan like fireflies and utterly deluded him*". However disappointing Magruder's subsequent wartime performance might have been, this remained his great moment, when almost single-handedly he stopped the advance of an invading army five times larger than his own.

The Clark House to the east of Yorktown was turned into the main hospital for Heintzelman's III Corps during the Siege of Yorktown. The York River can be seen in the distance, to the north of the house. During this stage of the campaign far more casualties were caused by disease than by enemy action. (Stratford Archive)

McClellan was disconcerted by the news that he clearly faced more men than he anticipated. He argued that not even an inexperienced commander like Magruder would attempt to hold a 12-mile line with just 15,000 men, so clearly the Confederates had been reinforced. This was the first serious overestimation of Confederate strength of the campaign, and far from the last. Worse still, a telegram from Washington informed him that McDowell's I Corps would be detached from the Army of the Potomac, as President Lincoln deemed it was needed to defend the capital. This was a grievous blow, as it robbed McClellan of some 42,000 men: reinforcements he had counted on when planning the whole campaign. He immediately wrote to Lincoln and Stanton to say that the decision imperiled the entire campaign, but the mind of the President was set. McClellan would have to fight Magruder and whoever else had reinforced him with the troops at his immediate disposal.

An 1861-pattern 13in. mortar dug in outside Yorktown during mid-April 1862. These Union weapons had a range of a mile and a half. (Stratford Archive)

His methodical plan to outflank Yorktown had been thwarted, so he clearly had to develop a new scheme. An engineer by training and mentality, McClellan opted for a siege. He gave orders to dig entrenchments facing the enemy line, then sent orders to improve the roads, then bring up the army's siege train, which was due to be landed at Fort Monroe. This decision gave the Confederates the time they needed to rush troops to the Richmond theater, and brought further criticism of McClellan from Washington and the press. A British military observer had been impressed by the decision to land his army behind Richmond to the east, describing it as "*the stride of a giant.*" After 5 April, the same observer described McClellan's advance to Yorktown as "*the step of a dwarf.*"

THE SIEGE OF YORKTOWN

During the next few weeks, McClellan continued to bombard Washington with demands that McDowell's Corps be returned to the Army of the Potomac. He even invented new uses for the formation, including an amphibious attack on Gloucester Point to gain access to

Union Mortar Battery 4, Looking westwards towards Yorktown, 16 April 1862. On the right, Gloucester Point can be seen across the York River. (Stratford Archive)

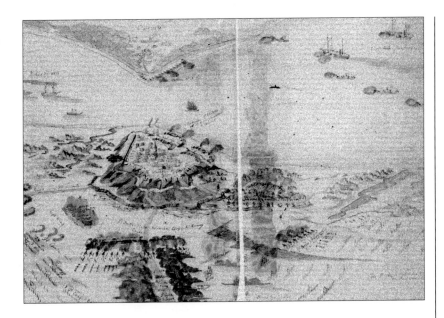

the York River, and further amphibious attacks upstream. All these schemes failed to sway Lincoln and Stanton.

Several senior officers in the army were in favor of probing the Confederate defenses. On 6 April, McClellan ordered Professor Thaddeus C. Lowe, the army's aeronautical specialist, to launch his hot air balloon *Intrepid,* in order to examine the Yorktown defenses. He achieved little, apart from giving Magruder a further opportunity to confuse the enemy. McClellan ordered his commanders to hold their positions. While this was going on, some 60 miles to the northwest the leading units of Johnston's army began to enter Richmond. The men were cheered through the streets, and were welcomed with offers of food and drink. Magruder was going to get his reinforcements. Actually, the first Confederate troops to join Magruder's men arrived from Norfolk, as General Huger (pronounced "Hew-jay") sent Magruder one of his brigades as soon as he heard of the Union landing. After a forced march from Richmond, the first two brigades of Johnston's Army arrived in Yorktown on 7 April, and another five brigades arrived over the next four days. This meant that by 11 April, Magruder commanded 34,400 men. Confederate observers expressed surprise that McClellan had permitted day after day to lapse without an assault. As Johnston put it in a letter to Robert E. Lee: "*no one but McClellan could have hesitated to attack.*"

After a brief visit to the front line on 12 April, when he inspected Magruder's lines along the Warwick River, Johnston returned to Richmond to tell President Davis that the defense of Magruder's line was impossible. This took place during a special conference, attended by the President and his senior commander as well as generals Robert E. Lee, Gustavus Smith, James Randolph and James Longstreet. Davies and Johnston distrusted each other, but the President was forced to give his army commander complete control over all Confederate forces in the region, including Magruder's and Huger's commands. He then sent the general to Yorktown, with clear orders to hold back the Union advance for as long as possible. Johnston was sure that McClellan would begin his assault within days, forcing President Davis to adopt Johnston's preferred strategy, which

43

was to fight a defensive battle on the outskirts of Richmond.

During the weeks after its arrival in front of Yorktown, the Army of the Potomac transported its siege guns and mortars from Washington to Fort Monroe by boat, then used barges to ship them up the York River to the front line under cover of darkness.

Both sides used their spades more than their muskets, as the Confederates strove to improve their defenses, while the Union troops were forced to dig new entrenchment lines from scratch a few hundred yards to the east. While this was taking place patrols and skirmishes as well as intermittent artillery duels became daily occurrences. Colonel Selden of the 7th Maine wrote that: *"There's scarcely a minute in the day when you cannot hear either the report of a field piece an explosion of a shell, or the crack of a rifle."* While this was not yet a formal siege, the two armies were now locked in a grim duel across the low marshy ground flanked by the two rivers. In sectors where such exchanges were rare, boredom was the real enemy. A soldier from Mississippi wrote that: *"This is the dullest place I ever saw, nothing to arouse one from the oppressive monotony of an occasional false alarm ... I am afraid we shall stay in this abominable swamp for a long time without a fight."* To add to the suffering, near-constant rain filled the trenches with mud and water, making life extremely unpleasant. This was a far cry from the romantic, glorious battle that the recruits of both sides had expected to fight.

Reinforcements brought the Confederate strength to around 50,000 men, while McClellan commanded twice that number. McClellan had the strength to storm his way through the Confederate line, but he was

Professor Thaddeus Lowe's largest military observation balloon *Intrepid* being prepared for a flight. The Army of the Potomac's Aeronautic Corps was extremely active during the Siege of Yorktown. (Library of Congress)

The ground crew of an observation balloon hauls down their craft following an observation flight near Yorktown in April 1862. In ideal conditions, at a height of 300ft, Lowe and his observers could see approximately 15 miles. (Library of Congress)

The Confederate "Water Battery" at Yorktown was designed to cover the city from attack via the York River. This sketch was made after the campaign, when the battery was held by Union troops. During the Siege of Yorktown, the Confederates deployed 8in. Columbiads in this position. (Stratford Archive)

reluctant to commit his army to such a potentially costly maneuver. He also regarded the Warwick River line as virtually impregnable, and concentrated on the Yorktown section of the Confederate defenses. After observing the siege of Sevastopol (1854–55) during the Crimean War, he regarded himself as an expert in siege operations. McClellan had no doubt about the outcome of the coming battle. He left Brigadier General Fitz-John Porter in charge of siege operations and work on Union fortifications, while "Little Mac" concentrated on his planning, and re-reading his notes and published studies from the Crimea.

Meanwhile, two incidents during the first week in April almost revealed the full extent of Magruder's deception. The first took place in their area between Yorktown and the headwaters of the Warwick River, where Hamilton's Division of Heintzelman's III Corps was stationed. Hamilton had discovered that the Confederate lines to his front were thinly defended, and both divisional and Corps commanders requested that McClellan allow them to conduct a reconnaissance in force. McClellan, supported by Porter and the army's Chief Engineer, John Barnard, rejected their proposal out of hand. On the Confederate right wing behind the Warwick River, near-constant rain favored the defenders, making the river an even greater obstacle. This did not deter Brigadier General William "Baldy" Smith, who sent Hancock's Brigade in a reconnaissance across the river on 6 April. Just as Hancock found a gap in the Confederate line on the western bank, orders arrived from Army Headquarters calling for all troops to dig in, and not to attack the enemy. If followed through, either or both of these operations could have led to the collapse of the Confederate line.

A more aggressive raid across the Warwick River was launched on 16 April, when McClellan approved plans for another foray across Dam No. 1, the location of Hancock's attack ten days before. In a skirmish that became known as the battle of Lee's Mill, the Confederates were forced to withdraw from the western bank after being pounded by Union batteries on the east side of the river. After three hours a small force of Union infantry (part of the 3rd Vermont) crossed the river and established a bridgehead on the far bank, but a prompt response by Confederate reserves saved the day. A sharp fight ensued, and the Union attackers withdrew. This was the only **45**

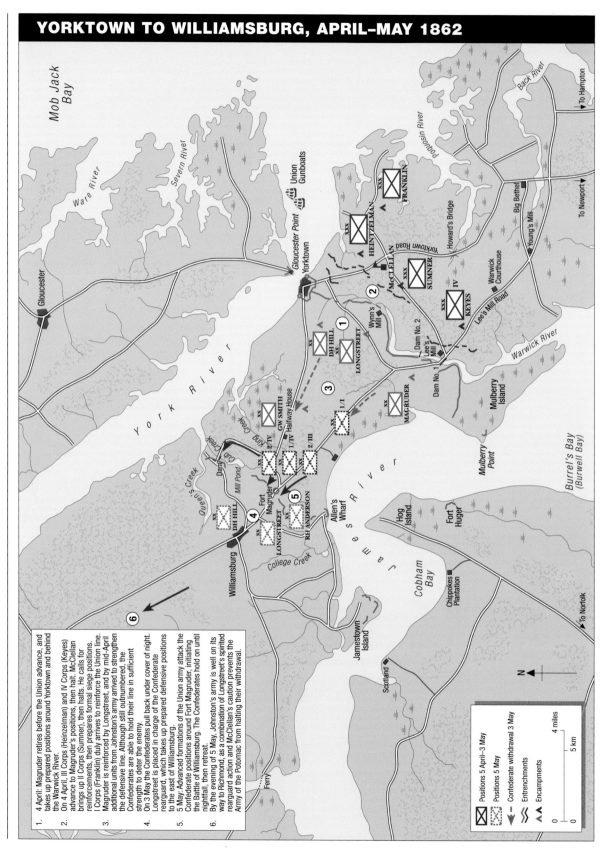

YORKTOWN TO WILLIAMSBURG, APRIL–MAY 1862

1. 4 April: Magruder retires before the Union advance, and takes up prepared positions around Yorktown and behind the Warwick River.
2. On 4 April, III Corps (Heintzelman) and IV Corps (Keyes) advance to Magruder's positions, then halt. McClellan brings up II Corps (Sumner), then prepares formal siege positions. I Corps (Franklin) duly arrives to reinforce the Union line. Magruder is reinforced by Longstreet, and by mid-April additional units from Johnston's army arrived to strengthen the defensive line. Although still outnumbered, the Confederates are able to hold their line in sufficient strength to deter the enemy.
3. On 3 May the Confederates pull back under cover of night. Longstreet is placed in charge of the Confederate rearguard, which takes up prepared defensive positions to the east of Williamsburg.
4. 5 May: Advanced formations of the Union army attack the Confederate positions around Fort Magruder, initiating the Battle of Williamsburg. The Confederates hold on until nightfall, then retreat.
5. By the evening of 5 May, Johnston's army is well on its way to Richmond, as a combination of Longstreet's spirited rearguard action and McClellan's caution prevents the Army of the Potomac from halting their withdrawal.

46

The southeastern portion of the Yorktown defenses, looking westwards towards the Nelson House, on the edge of the town itself. The dark strip in the center of the photograph marks the position of the road that ran southwards behind the line of Confederate entrenchments towards the James River. (Virginia Historical Society)

aggressive move that McClellan made during the four weeks his army sat in front of Yorktown.

The siege continued. Minor patrols and forays helped to provide some relief from the monotony of the siege, as did the cheering sight of balloon flights. At one point, the balloon operated by Professor Thaddeus Lowe broke its moorings while General Fitz-John Porter was on board. The balloon drifted over the Confederate lines, but disaster was averted when the wind changed, and the balloon drifted back to safety. The Confederates also deployed a balloon, launched from a barge on the James River that became a proto-aircraft carrier for a few weeks.

Despite harassing fire from Confederate guns in Yorktown, Union troops slowly advanced their siege works and emplaced their heavy artillery. The army's 101 siege guns included the latest Parrott rifled guns, plus numerous coastal guns, mainly 8in. or 10in. Rodman and Columbiad smoothbores. The siege train also included over 40 siege mortars, the largest being immense 13in. seacoast mortars, which fired 220lb mortar bombs. These weapons were ideally suited to pulverizing the Confederate

The same position photographed in the summer of 2003. The Nelson House is obscured by the trees lining the approach road to the Yorktown Battlefield Park Visitor Center. (Author's photograph)

ABOVE **The High Bastion marked the northeastern corner of the Confederate defenses around Yorktown. Built on top of a British redoubt dating from the Revolutionary War, this bastion could enfilade an enemy assaulting the main defensive line. In this photograph, taken in May 1862, the viewpoint is from the top of the river bluff, to the northeast of the Confederate position.**

LEFT **The interior of the High Bastion at Yorktown, looking towards the northeast. This photograph was taken in May 1862, after the defenses were abandoned by the Confederates. The Confederate rifled guns deployed in this position could have covered both the York River and the eastern approaches to the town. (US Army Military Historical Institute)**

defenses when the bombardment began. This arsenal represented the largest siege train ever deployed on American soil, and there was no doubt that when the guns and mortars opened fire, the Confederate defenses would be shattered. They were deployed to concentrate on the town defenses, plus a small section of the Confederate line to the south of the city. Meanwhile, two Union Corps were in place to assault the remains of the enemy defenses. McClellan was happy about the growing stockpile of shot, shell and bombs, and set the date for the commencement of his grand bombardment as 5 May. The US Navy was also called upon to prepare a naval bombardment from the York River to coincide with the attack. While "Little Mac" was criticized over his tardiness, nobody could fault his organizational skills. His siege would be a model operation, planned and prepared down to the last detail.

The only problem was, General Joseph Johnston was now in command of the Confederate defenses, and he was an expert in and an advocate of the timely withdrawal. He never considered the Yorktown line to be defensible, given McClellan's superiority in heavy ordnance. From 27 April on, preparations were made for a withdrawal before the Union bombardment began. Two days later he informed President Davis that the enemy siege lines and "parallels" were almost complete, writing: "*the fight for Yorktown, as I said in Richmond, must be one of artillery, in which we cannot win. The result is certain; the time only doubtfull ... I shall therefore move as soon as it can be done conveniently.*"

Withdrawal was no easy matter. By the start of May, Johnston had 56,600 men and around 150 guns under his command. Preparations were made under great secrecy. First, supplies and nonessential artillery were moved westward towards Richmond, followed by personal baggage. A runaway slave reported these developments to Union newspapermen, but McClellan chose not to believe the story, stating that he had firm intelligence that Johnston intended to stand and fight. By 3 May, everything was ready. A number of outdated heavy guns were abandoned due to lack of transport, but otherwise the preparations were made without incident. Then, on the evening of 3 May, the Confederate guns erupted in a barrage of Union positions that lasted almost until dawn. As General Early wrote: "*The object to this was to dispose of as much of the fixed ammunition as possible and produce the impression that we were preparing for an attack on their enemy's trenches.*"

The ruse worked like a charm, and the Confederate columns marched off to the west, followed by the artillery. Only Stuart's cavalry remained behind as a screen. To cover the retreat even further, dummy "quaker" guns made from painted logs and scarecrow sentries were left behind. Confederate engineers also rigged the area around Yorktown with "torpedoes" (mines) and booby-traps, designed to sow confusion amongst the enemy while they occupied the Confederate positions.

The interior of the High Bastion, photographed in the summer of 2003. The small artillery piece covering the outer face of the bastion is a replica piece of the Revolutionary War, and is in the same position as the large smoothbore piece in the previous photograph. (Author's photo)

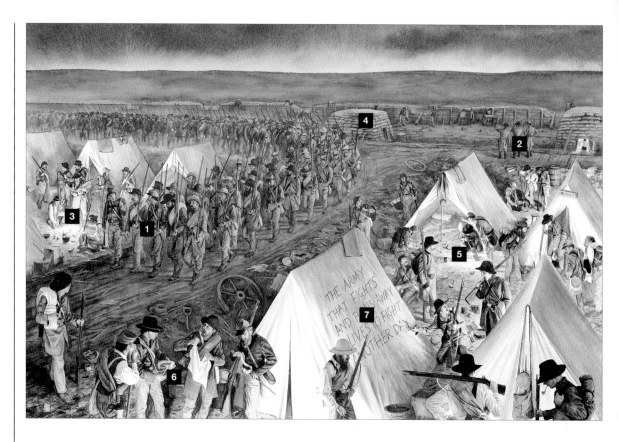

THE CONFEDERATE WITHDRAWAL FROM YORKTOWN
(pages 50–51)

By the start of May 1862, the small Confederate army charged with blocking McClellan's advance up Virginia's Tidewater Peninsula had managed to hold the enemy at bay for a whole month. A combination of deception on the part of Confederate General Magruder and caution by General McClellan meant that no serious attempt was made to force the Confederate defenses. Instead, McClellan laid siege to Yorktown, and prepared to launch a devastating artillery bombardment of the small port. Although Confederate numbers had increased, General Johnston, who now commanded the Confederate Army in the Peninsula was under no illusions. Aware of the Army of the Potomac's overwhelming superiority in artillery, he had little option but to make clandestine preparations for a withdrawal, timed to precede the start of the Union bombardment. On the night of 3 May, the Confederates crept away from their entrenchments, and headed west up the peninsula towards Williamsburg. This scene depicts the withdrawal. In the center a column of Confederate infantry (1) march throughout the encampment, heading towards the Williamsburg Road, which led to the west and safety. Confederate officers (2) supervise the emplacement of dummy sentries, "quaker guns" and the stoking of campfires (3) in an attempt to hide the withdrawal of the army from Union observers. Beyond the line of entrenchments the glow of Union campfires can be seen in the distance. After a month of siege, the Confederate entrenchments round Yorktown and stretching from the town south towards the Warwick River were fairly sophisticated; the works shown in this stretch include bomb-proof shelters (4), ready-use magazines and well-constructed gun emplacements. In addition to these deceptions, Confederate engineers prepared dozens of booby-traps or "mines" (5), which were scattered about the camp, designed to be detonated by Union soldiers when they occupied the Confederate encampment. These devices were relatively simple, involving small powder charges, percussion caps and tripwires. Most were buried, but others were placed inside camp paraphernalia, such as canteens, barrels and cooking utensils. Meanwhile, the Confederate rearguard prepare to withdraw, the men wrapping their equipment in sacking (6) to reduce noise, and even scrawling jeering messages for the Union troops who would inevitably occupy the camp the following day. A Union soldier recorded seeing this particular sentiment (7) written on the side of a tent the next morning. (Steve Noon)

The following morning (4 May) Thaddeus Lowe was sent aloft in his balloon to examine the Confederate positions. He reported that they appeared to be empty. Union patrols were quickly sent forward, and the report was confirmed. Johnston and his men had escaped, abandoning Yorktown only hours before McClellan's bombardment was due to begin. Naturally McClellan declared this to be a victory, telegraphing Washington with the news that; "*Yorktown is in our possession.*"

THE BATTLE OF WILLIAMSBURG

For all his faults, McClellan was not tardy in pursuit. After discovering the Confederates had withdrawn he ordered his cavalry to pursue, then sent his leading infantry formations forward to support his horsemen. The Union cavalry caught up with Johnston's rearguard just outside Williamsburg, where Magruder had built a secondary line of defense spanning the gap between small tributaries of the York and James rivers. Late in the afternoon of 4 May, a cavalry skirmish developed to the east of the town. After this initial clash, General Stoneman, the Union commander, decided to halt and wait for infantry support. The arrival of the infantry was delayed by mud and rain, but the men of Hooker's Division (2/III) finally arrived in front of the Confederate positions during the early hours of the following morning.

Realizing that his supply wagons and artillery needed more time to withdraw towards Richmond, Johnston made the decision to stand and fight. The Union army approached Williamsburg along two roads that converged immediately east of the town. This junction was covered by a large earthwork known as Fort Magruder. James Longstreet was in command of the Confederate rearguard, and he occupied this defensive work, along with other secondary positions on either side of the road into Williamsburg. An initial Union attack by Hooker's Division was repulsed during the morning, and a counterattack by Longstreet against the left flank of Hooker's position threatened to break the Union line. Around noon, General Sumner, the commander of II Corps, arrived to take charge of the battle, just as the divisions of W.H. Smith (2/IV) and Couch (1/IV) arrived along the northern road from Yorktown. Union scouts reported that the Confederates had not manned their entire line, as earthworks to the north of the battle arena appeared empty of troops. Sumner ordered Hancock's Brigade (1/2/IV) of W.F. Smith's Division to occupy these empty positions. By 3.00pm the aggressive Union commander was in possession of the enemy redoubts after crossing Cub Creek by way of the Mill Pond Dam. This move forced Longstreet to deploy his only reserve to counter this new threat: the brigade of Jubal Early (part of D.H. Hill's Division, sent back from the retreating columns to reinforce Longstreet). The Confederate brigade launched an uncoordinated attack against Hancock's position around 5.00pm, but the assault was repulsed with heavy casualties. Hancock ignored contradictory orders from Sumner to retreat back over the creek, and saved the day for the Union. D.H. Hill, riding up to see how Early fared, promptly ordered the attack broken off. To the south, the Confederate counterattack had pushed the Union line back onto the Lee's Mill Road, but the arrival of Kearny's Brigade (1/1/I) in mid-afternoon was

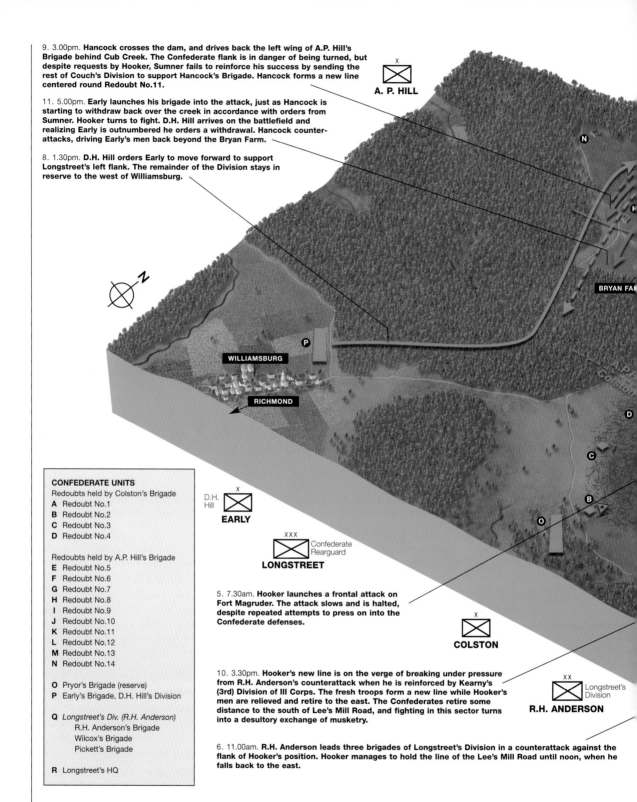

9. 3.00pm. Hancock crosses the dam, and drives back the left wing of A.P. Hill's Brigade behind Cub Creek. The Confederate flank is in danger of being turned, but despite requests by Hooker, Sumner fails to reinforce his success by sending the rest of Couch's Division to support Hancock's Brigade. Hancock forms a new line centered round Redoubt No.11.

11. 5.00pm. Early launches his brigade into the attack, just as Hancock is starting to withdraw back over the creek in accordance with orders from Sumner. Hooker turns to fight. D.H. Hill arrives on the battlefield and realizing Early is outnumbered he orders a withdrawal. Hancock counterattacks, driving Early's men back beyond the Bryan Farm.

8. 1.30pm. D.H. Hill orders Early to move forward to support Longstreet's left flank. The remainder of the Division stays in reserve to the west of Williamsburg.

A. P. HILL

N

BRYAN FAR

P

WILLIAMSBURG

RICHMOND

D

C

B

O

CONFEDERATE UNITS
Redoubts held by Colston's Brigade
A Redoubt No.1
B Redoubt No.2
C Redoubt No.3
D Redoubt No.4

Redoubts held by A.P. Hill's Brigade
E Redoubt No.5
F Redoubt No.6
G Redoubt No.7
H Redoubt No.8
I Redoubt No.9
J Redoubt No.10
K Redoubt No.11
L Redoubt No.12
M Redoubt No.13
N Redoubt No.14

O Pryor's Brigade (reserve)
P Early's Brigade, D.H. Hill's Division

Q Longstreet's Div. (R.H. Anderson)
    R.H. Anderson's Brigade
    Wilcox's Brigade
    Pickett's Brigade

R Longstreet's HQ

D.H. Hill
EARLY

Confederate Rearguard
LONGSTREET

COLSTON

Longstreet's Division
R.H. ANDERSON

5. 7.30am. Hooker launches a frontal attack on Fort Magruder. The attack slows and is halted, despite repeated attempts to press on into the Confederate defenses.

10. 3.30pm. Hooker's new line is on the verge of breaking under pressure from R.H. Anderson's counterattack when he is reinforced by Kearny's (3rd) Division of III Corps. The fresh troops form a new line while Hooker's men are relieved and retire to the east. The Confederates retire some distance to the south of Lee's Mill Road, and fighting in this sector turns into a desultory exchange of musketry.

6. 11.00am. R.H. Anderson leads three brigades of Longstreet's Division in a counterattack against the flank of Hooker's position. Hooker manages to hold the line of the Lee's Mill Road until noon, when he falls back to the east.

BATTLE OF WILLIAMSBURG
5 May 1862, viewed from the southeast. As McClellan's Army of the Potomac pushes towards Richmond, Longstreet's ad hoc rearguard fights a determined action to buy time for the Confederate army to withdraw in safety.

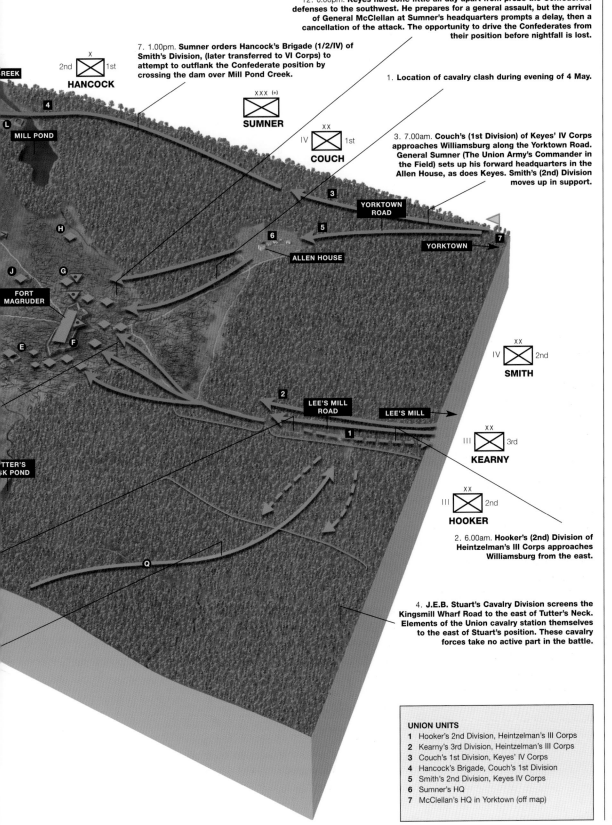

12. 6.00pm. Keyes has done little all day apart from probe the Confederate defenses to the southwest. He prepares for a general assault, but the arrival of General McClellan at Sumner's headquarters prompts a delay, then a cancellation of the attack. The opportunity to drive the Confederates from their position before nightfall is lost.

7. 1.00pm. Sumner orders Hancock's Brigade (1/2/IV) of Smith's Division, (later transferred to VI Corps) to attempt to outflank the Confederate position by crossing the dam over Mill Pond Creek.

1. Location of cavalry clash during evening of 4 May.

REEK

2nd ☒ 1st

HANCOCK

4

L

MILL POND

SUMNER
XXX (+)

IV ☒ 1st

COUCH
XX

3

3. 7.00am. Couch's (1st Division) of Keyes' IV Corps approaches Williamsburg along the Yorktown Road. General Sumner (The Union Army's Commander in the Field) sets up his forward headquarters in the Allen House, as does Keyes. Smith's (2nd) Division moves up in support.

YORKTOWN ROAD

5

6

ALLEN HOUSE

YORKTOWN

7

H

J

G

FORT MAGRUDER

E

F

IV ☒ 2nd

SMITH
XX

2

LEE'S MILL ROAD

LEE'S MILL

1

III ☒ 3rd

KEARNY
XX

TTER'S K POND

III ☒ 2nd

HOOKER
XX

2. 6.00am. Hooker's (2nd) Division of Heintzelman's III Corps approaches Williamsburg from the east.

Q

4. J.E.B. Stuart's Cavalry Division screens the Kingsmill Wharf Road to the east of Tutter's Neck. Elements of the Union cavalry station themselves to the east of Stuart's position. These cavalry forces take no active part in the battle.

UNION UNITS
1 Hooker's 2nd Division, Heintzelman's III Corps
2 Kearny's 3rd Division, Heintzelman's III Corps
3 Couch's 1st Division, Keyes' IV Corps
4 Hancock's Brigade, Couch's 1st Division
5 Smith's 2nd Division, Keyes IV Corps
6 Sumner's HQ
7 McClellan's HQ in Yorktown (off map)

Union troops entering Yorktown, 4 May 1862, viewed from the west. The Nelson House can be seen on the right side of the road, while the small jetties along the York River can be seen below the river bluffs on the left of the picture. (Stratford Archive)

enough to stem the Confederate advance. Darkness brought an end to the fighting. This was a confusing battle for both armies, fought amidst mud and rain, but at least Longstreet had bought Johnston the time he needed to pull his army back to safety.

Both sides claimed victory at Williamsburg. Longstreet withdrew during the night, allowing McClellan to claim that he captured the enemy positions, and he proclaimed the skirmish "a brilliant victory." The truth was he allowed Johnston to slip away.

From Williamsburg to Seven Pines

When McClellan occupied Yorktown he decided to augment his advance up the Peninsula with an amphibious attack. West Point lay on a peninsula created by the confluence of the Pamunkey, Mattapony and York rivers, and was the terminus of the Richmond & York River Railroad. Two brigades of William Franklin's Division (1/I) were embarked on transports during 6 May, then sent up the York River to occupy West Point. The following morning Franklin disembarked the bulk of his force at Eltham's Landing, a plantation on the south bank of the York River. Rather than advance to block Johnston's line of retreat to Richmond, Franklin elected to dig in. To protect his retreating columns, Johnston sent John Bell Hood's Texas Brigade to pin Franklin. The two forces met during the afternoon of 7 May, and despite being outnumbered the Texans drove the Union line back almost into the river. Johnston later asked Hood what his Texans would have done if the order had been to attack the enemy rather than just pin them. Hood replied; "*I suppose, General, they would have driven them into the river, and tried to swim out and capture the gunboats.*"

Johnston's retreat caused consternation in Richmond. Refugees fleeing the Union advance filled the city, while others fled Richmond and headed west or south. Each day brought McClellan and his invaders closer to the Confederate capital, and for all his abilities, Johnston appeared as reluctant as McClellan to stand and fight. Appalling roads and a lack of supplies made the retreat difficult, while the troops themselves found it hard to understand why so much territory should be ceded without a fight. When Johnston reached the hamlet of Barhamsville he divided the army. Longstreet and D.H. Hill crossed the Chickahominy River at Long Bridge while the rest of the army

Fort Magruder to the east of Williamsburg dominated the roads leading into the town from Lee's Mill and Yorktown. The defenders felled a swathe of trees in front of the position to provide a clear field of fire. View from the east. Williamsburg can be seen in the distance. (Stratford Archive)

Union troops of Brigadier General Philip Kearny's Brigade (1/1/I) sketched while marching to reinforce Brigadier General Joseph Hooker's Division during the battle of Williamsburg, 5 May 1862. Sketch by Alfred Waud for *Harper's Weekly*. (Library of Congress)

continued its retreat along the Williamsburg Stage Road. The closer the army came to Richmond the better its supply situation became, but still the retreat continued. The Confederate commander seemed obsessed with extracting his army rather than defending his capital. Johnston revealed something of this obsession on 10 May when he wrote: "*the folly of sending his army down the peninsula is only equalled by our good fortune in getting away from there.*" On 12 May, President Davis and Robert E. Lee rode out to meet Johnston to discuss the situation. What they discovered alarmed both men. It seemed as if the Confederate commander had no coherent plan to defend the capital at all, forcing Davis and Lee to call a meeting of the Virginia Assembly two days later. There, Davis and Lee both declared that Richmond must be held at all costs. Johnston could retreat no further. McClellan also received a visit from his superiors, when President Lincoln and Edwin Stanton arrived at Fort Monroe to discover more about the situation in the Peninsula. They arrived just in time to learn of the Confederate abandonment of Norfolk, a withdrawal forced by Johnston's retreat, and the need to gather all available troops around Richmond to defend the city. Late on 10 May, Union troops occupied the Confederate port, and just hours later the crew of the Confederate ironclad *Virginia* (formerly the *Merrimac*) were forced to

McCLELLAN'S ADVANCE TO THE CHICKAHOMINY, MAY 1862

1. Johnston's Confederates retreat to Richmond after the Battle of Williamsburg (5 May), reaching positions around the capital ten days later.
2. McClellan advances slowly up the peninsula, probing the Confederate rearguard, but never moving fast enough to catch Johnston.
3. Franklin's Corps is transported up the York River by steamer, and lands south of West Point on 7 May. G.W. Smith's Division is sent to block his advance up the Pamunkey River, and a small action is fought before the Confederates withdraw. West Point then becomes the Union forward supply depot, and Franklin's corps moves west to secure the White House, and then joins McClellan's main advance.
4. 27 May: Porter's V Corps engages Confederate forces in a small-scale battle near Hanover Junction. The Confederates are outnumbered and defeated in an engagement which McClellan proclaims a major victory. Porter then consolidates his position to the north of the Chickahominy River, along Beaver Dam Creek.
5. By late May Franklin's VI Corps reaches the Chickahominy River at New Bridge, and takes up defensive positions on the north bank of the river.
6. Keyes IV Corps crosses the Chickahominy River at Bottom's Bridge and takes up an advanced position around Seven Pines and Fair Oaks. Heinzelman's III Corps moved up behind him into reserve positions around Bottom's Bridge and Savage's Station.
7. Johnston's army continues to improve its defensive positions around Richmond, and probes to the north in an effort to maintain rail communications along the Virginia Central Railroad.

Confederate defensive positions late May 1862.

Supply Depot
Fort Monroe

Hampton

Hampton Roads

Mob Jack Bay

Rappahannock

Urbanna

Piankatonk

York River

Yorktown

Halfway House

Lee's Mill

Williamsburg

James River

Surrey Courthouse

King & Queen's Courthouse

Supply Depot

West Point

VI FRANKLIN
xxx

Army of the Potomac

XXXX McCLELLAN

Richmond & York River Railroad

King William Courthouse

White House

III HEINTZELMAN
xxx

New Kent Courthouse

Chickahominy

Pamunkey

Jones Bridge

St Mary's Church

Charles City Courthouse

Blackwater

Bottom's Bridge

Long Bridge

V PORTER
xxx

VI FRANKLIN
xxx

IV KEYES
xxx

Hanover

Old Cold Harbour

Cold Harbour

New Bridge

Seven Pines

White Oak Creek

Malvern Hill

Norfolk & Petersburg Railroad

Hanover Junction

Gaine's Mill

New Bridge

New Market

Mechanicsville

Meadow Bridge

Mechanicsville Bridge

Richmond

Drewry's Bluff

Virginia Central Railroad

Richmond & Fredericksburg & Potomac Railroad

Richmond & Danville RR

Richmond & Petersburg Railroad

Petersburg

Appomattox

Weldon & Petersburg Railroad

N

20 miles
25 km

58

White House on the Pamunkey River became the forward supply base of the Army of the Potomac as McClellan advanced up the Peninsula from Williamsburg to the Chickahominy River. (Stratford Archive)

scuttle their ship. The Union Navy now controlled the waters of both the James and the York rivers.

Flag Officer Goldsborough ordered a Union naval force to advance up the James River, with orders to bombard Richmond into submission. The only real obstacle in their path was a Confederate battery of eight heavy guns at Drewry's Bluff, a 100ft-high escarpment overlooking a bend in the James River from its southern bank, some seven miles below Richmond. Pilings and block-ships barred the river below the fort, while sharpshooters lined the banks. On 15 May, Commander John Rogers led his squadron against the Confederate position. At his disposal were the ironclads USS *Monitor* and USS *Galena*, plus two wooden gunboats (*Port Royal* and *Aroostook*), and the experimental ironclad vessel *Naugatuck*. Unable to elevate their guns sufficiently to hit the Confederate positions on top of the Bluff, the Union warships were subjected to plunging fire from above, where their armor was weakest. After three hours of this unequal contest Rogers called off the attack. The battered Union warships limped back to Hampton Roads to report that the back door to Richmond had been bolted[2].

---

2 See Campaign 103 *Hampton Roads 1862 – First clash of the Ironclads*, p.89

The Railroad Bridge over the Pamunkey River was quickly repaired by Union engineers, and the Richmond & York River Railroad was pressed into service to haul Union supplies to the army encamped astride the Chickahominy River. Note the railroad engine on a barge in the background; another example of the phenomenal logistical resources available to McClellan. (National Archives)

The same day, Johnston ordered his army to withdraw behind the Chickahominy River, bringing the Confederates to the outskirts of Richmond. The River was: *"a narrow, sluggish stream, flowing through swampland covered with a rank, dense, tangled growth of trees, reeds, grasses and water plants."* It was also a formidable obstacle. Meanwhile, McClellan moved his forward base from Yorktown to the White House on the Pamunkey River, and preparations were made for the final stage of the advance. The White House became an enormous depot, and the advancing Union troops were able to capture the Richmond and York River Railroad virtually intact. Although McClellan later argued that he planned to use the James River as his base, the Union defeat at Drewry's Bluff persuaded him that the York River was the safer base of operations for his army. The Union advance towards the Chickahominy had been slow, hindered by appalling roads and mud. One soldier reported seeing an army mule sunk so far into the mud that only its ears were visible, and the advance was limited to some three or four miles per day. Finally, on 20 May, Casey's Division of Keyes' IV Corps reached the Chickahominy at Bottoms Bridge, on the Williamsburg Road, some 12 miles east of Richmond. The Union troops forded the river, and engineers began to repair the destroyed bridge. The following day McClellan arrived, and expressed surprise that the Confederates had not contested the line of the river. He gave orders that Keyes' IV Corps continue across the river to take a position six miles away at Seven Pines, to form the anchor of his left flank. Days later, Heintzelman's III Corps would also cross onto the south bank of the river. The Union advance continued on the north bank of the river until, on 24 May, Smith's Division (2/VI) of Franklin's VI Corps reached Mechanicsville, some five miles north of Richmond, a point that became the army's right flank. V Corps and II Corps halted behind Franklin, on the north bank of the river, and began work on improving the river crossings.

While all this was happening, great strategic changes were taking place. Earlier that summer, Robert E. Lee had sent General "Stonewall" Jackson to the Shenandoah Valley in an attempt to pin the Union forces there. Jackson's attack on General Banks at Kernstown (23 March) had so alarmed Washington that it temporarily abandoned its plans to send McDowell's I Corps to reinforce McClellan. After weeks of pressure from "Little Mac", Lincoln had finally agreed to release McDowell again, allowing him to march south through Fredericksburg to link up with McClellan. To protect his reinforcements, McClellan decided to keep the bulk of his army on the north bank of the Chickahominy River, and to send a probe north towards Hanover to join forces with McDowell when he arrived. Then, on 24 May, McClellan learned that McDowell's troops had been recalled a second time, because Jackson had defeated the Union forces in the Shenandoah at Front Royal. McClellan was furious, but he still hoped that the delay was only a temporary one. Consequently he sent Porter's V Corps north to cut the Virginia Central Railroad at Hanover Junction, responding to reports that a Confederate force had stationed itself there, between McClellan's and McDowell's forces. On 27 May Confederate Brigadier General Lawrence Branch of Gustavus Smith's Division occupied Hanover Junction with 4,000 men, charged with guarding the railroad. Porter advanced the bulk of his forces towards Hanover itself, but sent a small force to screen the railroad. Branch decided to attack, only to find he was heavily outnumbered. As more Union troops reached the scene, the Confederates were forced to withdraw. Inevitably, McClellan called the skirmish; "*a glorious victory over superior numbers.*" In fact, all the action had achieved was to fix the Union commander's attention to the north of the Chickahominy River. While this skirmish was taking place, plans were being laid for a Confederate assault that would threaten the Army of the Potomac with destruction. The result would be the bloody battle of Fair Oaks.

THE BATTLE OF FAIR OAKS

I n the early hours of 31 May, the Confederate army moved into position. Trooper Adams of Stuart's cavalry recalled: "*Saturday morning, the 31st was dull and wet … the roads were flooded, the woods were weeping.*" It was an inauspicious day to launch a major offensive. Most of Major General Daniel H. Hill's troops had got under way before dawn, heading east along the Williamsburg Road. His Division consisted of four brigades: those of Brigadier Samuel Garland, Brigadier Robert Rodes, Brigadier Gabriel Rains, and Colonel George B. Anderson (commanding Featherstone's Brigade). The original plan was for Hill to lead the Confederate assault with three of his brigades, while Rodes operated on the flank, hooking round on the Union defenses from the Charles City Road while the rest of the Division attacked from the east. Hill's initial assault would be followed up by Brigadier General Benjamin Huger's Division, which would follow on behind. Brigadier General William H.C. Whiting's and Major General James Longstreet's divisions would attack down the Nine Mile Road. The plan went awry from the beginning.

On the Nine Mile road to the north, Whiting (commanding Major General Gustavus Smith's Division) reached his start-line position at the Old Tavern at 6.00am but there was no sign of Longstreet. General Joseph E. Johnston had ordered Longstreet to attack down the Nine Mile Road towards the Williamsburg Road. Longstreet had misunderstood his orders, and thought he had to move from the Nine Mile Road to the Williamsburg Road before launching his attack. Consequently at dawn his division was at Gillies Creek, still well behind the Confederate lines, heading towards D.H. Hill's start-line on the Williamsburg Road west of Seven Pines. The creek was swollen by rain, forcing Longstreet to bridge the stream using a wagon covered with a trestle. This all took time, and to

The engagement at Drewry's Bluff (15 May 1862) when Confederate gunners prevented the Union fleet from advancing up the James River to Richmond. The ironclads USS *Monitor* (second from left) and USS *Galena* (third from left) are shown leading the attack on the Confederate position. (Friends of the Navy Memorial Museum)

The left flank of the Union army on the west bank of the Chickahominy River was anchored on the White Oak Swamp. Brigadier General Heintzelman's III Corps held this southern flank of the Union army until called upon to support Keyes' IV Corps at Fair Oaks. Photograph by James Gibson, May 1862. (Library of Congress)

complicate matters, Huger's Division arrived on the scene, adding to the congestion. The attack was supposed to have been launched at 6.00am. It was 9.00am by the time Longstreet's troops were formed up in column again on the south side of Gillies Creek, and Huger's men still had to cross, even though they were expected to join D.H. Hill's men in the assault, or support them from the southern flank. Hill would fight alone.

On the Williamsburg Road, the tail end of D.H. Hill's column became entangled with the forward elements of Longstreet's Division, so it was 11.00am before Hill's men were clear of the tangle and moving towards their form-up positions on the Williamsburg Road. Longstreet then had to let Huger's men pass him as they marched south down the Charles City Road, so it was noon before Longstreet's men were free to march east behind Hill on the Williamsburg Road. It was an inauspicious start to the attack.

Longstreet had six brigades under his command, but he detached three (those of Brigadier Cadmus M. Wilcox, Brigadier Raleigh E. Colson, and Brigadier Roger A. Pryor) under Wilcox's command and sent them after Huger, with orders to work their way around the Union flank, somewhere south of the Williamsburg Road. Similarly Brigadier George E. Pickett's Brigade was ordered to break off into the dense waterlogged woods to the left, head towards the railroad and protect the flank of both Hill and Longstreet. This left just two brigades (those of Colonel James L. Kemper and Brigadier Richard H. Anderson) to support D.H. Hill's attack.

Johnston learned of Longstreet's mistake around 10.00am, and sent couriers off to find out where his missing division had disappeared to. He also realized that Whiting was left alone on the Nine Mile Road, but seemed reluctant to commit Brigadier General Lafayette McLaws' Division to the attack, which was easily within range, and could be re-deployed with little risk of exposing Richmond to an immediate attack from the north. Whiting alone would take Longstreet's place, leading the northern arm of Johnston's two-pronged attack.

Whiting had five brigades at his disposal: those of Colonel Evander M. Law (commanding Whiting's own brigade), Brigadier Robert Hatton, Brigadier Wade Hampton, Brigadier John B. Hood, and Brigadier James J. Pettigrew. From his position around the Old Tavern he marched his columns a mile down the Nine Mile Road towards Fair Oaks Station. The road was little more than a river of mud, and progress was slow. By 1.00pm his leading troops were still a mile from the station. Reluctant to commit his men before Hill launched his attack, Whiting ordered his men to rest their arms and wait.

Meanwhile, Union Brigadier General Silas Casey was becoming concerned, as his pickets reported movement along the Williamsburg Road to the west. That morning he had pushed his picket line forward into the woods ahead of the clearing where his division was concentrated. Behind this picket line on the north side of the road was an abatis, covered by three of the five regiments of Brigadier Henry M. Naglee's Brigade (1/2/IV) and Spratt's New York Battery. The other two regiments were sent forward of the abatis to support the pickets. To the south of the road, three regiments of Brigadier Innis N. Palmer's New York Brigade (3/2/IV) were drawn up in the open ground, while his remaining regiment was stationed behind his front line, in front of Casey's Redoubt. The pentagonal redoubt itself was open at the rear, but presented a formidable obstacle to any attacker, as the eight guns inside it had a clear field of fire across the open ground to their front. A line of rifle pits stretched away to the south as far as the woods, and north to cross the Williamsburg Road. These were held by the men of Brigadier Henry W. Wessells' Brigade (2/2/IV). A mile to the east along the Williamsburg Road the other part of IV Corps, Brigadier General Darius N. Couch's Division was busy deploying into line at Seven Pines, protected by a second abatis line. Couch's Division consisted of three brigades; those of Brigadier John J. Peck, Brigadier John J. Abercrombie, and Brigadier Charles Devens. Peck drew up on the south side of the road, while Devens' men lined the earthworks blocking the road itself. Abercrombie was sent north along the Nine Mile Road, to screen the right flank of the Union position. The commander of IV Corps, Brigadier General Erasmus D. Keyes, was well aware that his right wing was vulnerable to an attack launched along the Nine Mile Road from Richmond, but he had no more troops to spare. For the moment, Abercrombie would have to hold off any attacks from that direction. Keyes was reasonably confident that his left flank was secure, as it rested on the impassable morass of White Oak Swamp. Also, Brigadier General Samuel P. Heintzelman's III Corps was supposed to be guarding the line of the swamp, with Brigadier General Joseph Hooker's Division concentrated north of the White Oak Bridge. He also expected Brigadier General Edwin Sumner's II Corps to be moving into position on his right flank, unaware that the Chickahominy River crossings were proving treacherous, and that Sumner's troops were still on the wrong side of the river. IV Corps was out on a limb, and a coordinated Confederate attack that morning could have destroyed it completely. Fortunately for Keyes, the confusion between Johnston and Longstreet meant that the chances of launching a coordinated attack were slipping away.

By 1.00pm Hill was ready to attack. He fired a gun as a signal to Longstreet and Whiting, then gave the order to advance. Rodes' Brigade had returned from its diversion down the Charles City Road when it was relieved by Huger's Division, so Hill had all four of his brigades available. Two brigades were formed up in line on either side of the Williamsburg Road; Garland supported by R.H. Anderson, and Rodes to the south supported by Rains. Garland's men waded over a small creek and struggled on through the woods towards the clearing ahead of them, driving in the startled Union pickets as they did so. In places his men were struggling waist deep in the water, but somehow they managed to maintain their order, and fell upon the first of Naglee's regiments, sited in front of the abatis on the edge of the clearing. The raw Union troops ran almost without firing a shot, and Garland's men swept on through the abatis to engage the Union line beyond. Ahead of him lay Spratt's Battery, whose fire managed to stem the Confederate advance, at least for a few minutes. Garland's men hugged the abatis while cannister scythed over them before the second wave of

Brigadier General W.H.C. Whiting commanded the Confederate left wing at the battle of Fair Oaks, and his troops launched several unsuccessful assaults against Brigadier General Sumner's II Corps north of the Nine Mile Road. (Stratford Archive)

Major General Daniel H. Hill was an aggressive commander; the ideal man to spearhead the attack by the Confederate right wing at the battle of Fair Oaks. Although known for his rashness, he concurred with Major General Longstreet on 1 June, and called off his attack after it encountered a reinforced Union line. (Valentine Museum, Richmond)

Confederate troops appeared at the edge of the clearing, and slightly to the north. Colonel John B. Gordon, a Confederate officer, recalled the scene: "*Reforming my men under a galling fire and ordering them forward in another charge upon the supporting lines, which fought with the most stubborn resistance, disputing every foot of ground.*" G.B. Anderson's Brigade pushed three regiments forward across the abatis to join Garland, while another regiment worked round to the left, to outflank the remaining advanced regiment of Naglee's command. This Confederate regiment then came under pressure from Naglee's main line, which had formed up around Spratt's Battery. Also, Abercrombie sent two of his regiments forward from the Nine Mile Road, pinning G.B. Anderson's isolated regiment in the boggy woods to the north of the clearing, then driving it back towards the west. For a while it seemed as if the whole Confederate attack would grind to a halt. A soldier in a Carolina company remembered afterwards that: "*my Captain, D.H. Hall, and about ten others of my company were all that were left of us … we did what shooting we could while laying on the ground amongst our dead and wounded comrades.*" The time was about 1.40pm.

At that moment Rodes' men emerged from the clearing south of the Williamsburg Road, and after dressing their ranks they advanced towards Palmer's Brigade, drawn up in a line in the open to the south of Naglee's troops. Rodes' front line of Alabama troops halted in front of Palmer's line, and a sharp firefight developed. Once again the attackers seemed reluctant to close with the enemy. Seeing his advance beginning to stall, D.H. Hill ordered Carter's Battery to move round onto Rodes' right flank, to provide supporting fire. The Union line still held its ground, so Hill deployed his reserve, Rains' Brigade, sending them round the southern flank of Rodes behind Carter and his guns. This did the trick, and the additional firepower made Palmer's men waver, then fall back. Rodes ordered his men to charge, and in a moment the Union line

A Union sharpshooter taking cover behind a tree trunk during the Peninsula Campaign. Union skirmishers kept up a sporadic fire against the left wing of D.H. Hill's Division at Seven Pines before being driven back by Confederate reinforcements later that afternoon. (Stratford Archive)

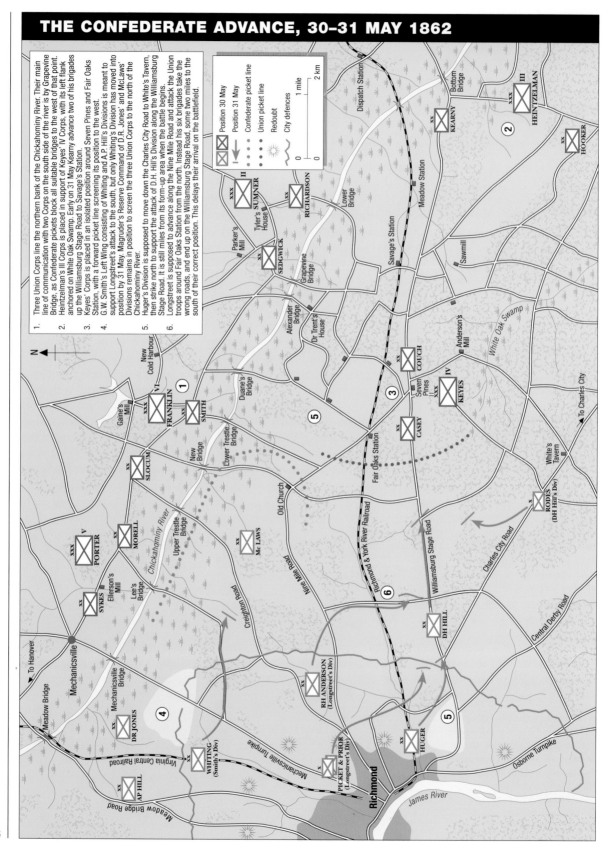

THE CONFEDERATE ADVANCE, 30–31 MAY 1862

1. Three Union Corps line the northern bank of the Chickahominy River. Their main line of communication with two Corps on the south side of the river is by Grapevine Bridge, as Confederate pickets block all suitable bridges to the west of that point.

2. Heintzelman's III Corps is placed in support of Keyes' IV Corps, with its left flank anchored on White Oak Swamp. Early on 31 May Kearny advance two of his brigades up the Williamsburg Stage Road to Savage's Station.

3. Keyes' Corps is placed in an isolated position around Seven Pines and Fair Oaks Station, with a forward picket line screening its position to the west.

4. G. W. Smith's Left Wing consisting of Whiting and A.P. Hill's Divisions is meant to support Longstreet's attack to the south, but only Whiting's Division has moved into position by 31 May. Magruder's Reserve Command of D.R. Jones' and McLaws' Divisions remains in position to screen the three Union Corps to the north of the Chickahominy River.

5. Huger's Division is supposed to move down the Charles City Road to White's Tavern, then strike north to support the attack of D.H. Hill's Division along the Williamsburg Stage Road. It is still miles from its form-up area when the battle begins.

6. Longstreet is supposed to advance along the Nine Mile Road and attack the Union troops around Fair Oaks Station from the north. Instead his six brigades take the wrong roads, and end up on the Williamsburg Stage Road, some two miles to the south of their correct position. This delays their arrival on the battlefield.

Legend:
- Position 30 May
- Position 31 May
- Confederate picket line
- Union picket line
- Redoubt
- City defences

0 1 mile
0 1 2 km

dissolved, as Palmer's men fled to the rear, hotly pursued by the Confederates. Rains and Carter turned their attention to the Union troops in Casey's Redoubt, and in the rifle pits on either side of it. They hardly needed to bother, as when the routing troops of Palmer's Brigade reached the Union entrenchments, they swept the men of Wessells' Brigade away with them. A few hardy souls remained to fire on the oncoming Confederate line, but within minutes Rodes had carried the redoubt, capturing eight Union guns abandoned inside it. Beyond lay a Union encampment. A Confederate soldier later wrote: "*We got a good many cannon and small arms ... we took between 500 and 1,000 prisoners ... we got a great many provisions of all kinds, bacon, flour, coffee ... besides several barrels of whiskey, one of which had a bullethole in it, from which several of the men filled their canteens.*" With two Union brigades in full retreat, the battle seemed to be turning Hill's way. Things continued to go badly for the men of Keyes' Corps. As Rodes' men reached the Union encampment grouped around the twin houses behind the redoubt, Brigadier General Couch in the second Union line realized that things had gone seriously wrong. He ordered a regiment of Devens' Brigade to advance beyond the line of the second abatis, to cover the retreat. This was another mistake, as when the mass of routing Union troops reached them, this regiment was carried away as well. As the men of Palmer's and Wessells' brigades threaded their way through the second abatis they lost all cohesion, and their rout became unstoppable. Couch ordered his men to pull aside to let the routers through, which did little to improve the morale of his men. Of Casey's Division, only Naglee's hard-pressed brigade remained on the field. The time was now around 2.30pm.

Rodes continued his pursuit through the second abatis line, but his men were now outstripping the rest of the division, and were becoming dangerously isolated. Couch sent two regiments of Peck's Brigade into the woods to the south of his position, in an attempt to enfilade the oncoming Confederates. Fortunately for Rodes, Carter's Battery had been keeping

67

pace with his advance, and unlimbered within yards of the enemy. The Confederates drove the Union troops back with cannister, forcing them to retreat in disorder. The Reverend Stewart, a Union Chaplain, witnessed the scene: "*Away went the boys with a shout, yet into what a fearful place were they so quickly hurried … A scene of horrid carnage immediately ensued. To fall back soon became a necessity, else either all be killed or taken prisoners.*" The crisis was averted, but what Rodes really needed was more troops, but Garland's and G.B. Anderson's Brigades were still locked in their fight with Naglee's troops, while for some reason Rains' Brigade remained on the southern flank of Casey's Redoubt. Rodes was unsupported, and the entrenched Union troops to his front outnumbered him two to one. Colonel Gordon described the situation: "*Nearly or quite half the line officers of* [my] *12 companies had by this time fallen dead or wounded … As I rode up and down my line … I passed my younger brother, only 19 years old, but the Captain of one of the companies. He was shot through the lungs and was bleeding profusely. I did not stop; I could not stop, nor would he permit me to stop.*" The Union musketry was also becoming stronger, and soon heavy fire prevented Rodes from advancing any further against the men of Devens' Brigade. Worse still, a messenger from Carter's Battery reported fresh Union troops were approaching from the south. This was Brigadier H.C. Berry's 3rd Brigade of Brigadier Philip Kearny's Division (3/III). Kearny had moved up behind Heintzelman's Corps during the morning, and by noon Berry's Brigade along with that of Brigadier D.B. Birney had reached Savage's Station. While Birney was ordered to advance to the northwest along the line of the Richmond & York River Railroad, Berry was sent around the southern flank of Couch's position. There is no evidence that Birney advanced any distance up the railroad, and remained in the vicinity of Savage's Station for the remainder of the day. When Brigadier C.D. Jameson's Brigade arrived, Kearny accompanied it as it followed Berry's men. It was 4.00pm before Berry reached his assigned position just south of Seven Pines, and he moved up to link with the Couch's left wing. When Jameson arrived, Kearny fitted his brigade into the line to Berry's left, and the division moved forward. Warned of its approach, Rodes re-deployed part of his brigade to face the new Union force, and soon Kearny's men were engaged in a brisk firefight with the Confederate troops of Rodes and Rains, supported by Carter's Battery. Rodes was already suffering heavy casualties from Couch's troops to his front, and was pinned down in the boggy ground around the abatis, and in the woods immediately to the south. This fresh action all but destroyed his brigade, and when Rodes himself was wounded, the situation became critical. Colonel John B. Gordon assumed temporary command of the brigade when Rodes was carried to the rear. At that crucial moment help arrived in the form of Colonel James L. Kemper, who brought up his brigade (part of Longstreet's Division), and plugged it into the line in front of the abatis. This allowed Gordon to redeploy more of his troops to face Berry, and pull his more shattered regiments to the rear.

While this fight was raging south of the Williamsburg Road, Garland and G.B. Anderson were making slow progress on the northern side of the turnpike. When the rest of Casey's Division turned and ran, Naglee held his men together, and during the afternoon they gave ground slowly, keeping the Confederates at bay until they reached the second abatis line. Naglee re-formed his brigade behind this barrier, and managed to prevent any further advance by Garland or G.B. Anderson. The fighting was fierce. A Union observer later wrote: "*Thousands of muskets in streaming volleys, with the sonorous roar of cannon and the hoarse screams of the combatants, created an uproar as if fiends had been unleashed to prey on each other. Storms of bullets and cannister tore wide passages through the trees and mangled the bodies of men.*" Just when it looked as if the Confederate advance had ground to a complete halt, R.H. Anderson appeared with a fresh brigade, commanded by Colonel Jenkins. This new unit drove forward into the woods to the north of the clearing, driving back Abercrombie's Brigade, then wheeling right to cut across the Nine Mile Road above Seven Pines. With Abercrombie in retreat, R.H. Anderson and Jenkins passed through the abatis northeast of the crossroads, then fell on the right flank of Devens' Brigade, drawn up behind the Seven Pines entrenchments. This was the chance Kemper had been waiting for, and he joined in the advance. Couch's remaining troops turned on their heels and fled, and the Confederates found themselves in possession of the Seven Pines crossroads. Couch's men retired eastward down the Williamsburg Road towards Savage's Station, but Hill's and Longstreet's men were too tired to pursue. This rout also brought about the retreat of Kearny's two brigades, who were wary of being cut off from support. They pulled back to the southeast, leaving Rains' and Gordon's men in possession of the battlefield.

While D.H. Hill and James Longstreet were occupied in the fight against Erasmus Keyes' IV Corps south of the Richmond & York River Railroad, Whiting was embroiled in another private battle to the north of the Nine Mile Road. Since 1.00pm his men had waited for orders to attack down the Nine Mile Road from Old Church, but the order never came. For some reason, the growing sound of battle to the south never carried that far north during the early afternoon, so Whiting was unaware that Hill's attack had begun. Finally, at 3.00pm, the sound of artillery fire was heard to the south. The sound also reached Johnston's headquarters, but the Confederate commander still thought Hill was engaged in an artillery duel, not a full-scale battle. While Whiting was raring to lead his men into action, Johnston continued to hold him back. It was not until a report from Longstreet reached Johnston's

Brigadier General Henry M. Naglee's Brigade (1/2/IV) was deployed to the west of Brigadier General Casey's main line, and was therefore the first Union formation to encounter D.H. Hill's Division when the Confederate attack began. (Stratford Archive)

Battery B, 1st New York Light Artillery Regiment (Captain Rufus D. Pettit) was attached to Richardson's (1st) Division of Sumner's II Corps during the battle of Fair Oaks. During 1 June 1862 the battery was positioned at the apex of the Union line, beside the railroad near Fair Oaks Station. This photograph was taken after the battle, when this position had been turned into a formidable entrenched position called Fort Richardson. (Virginia War Museum)

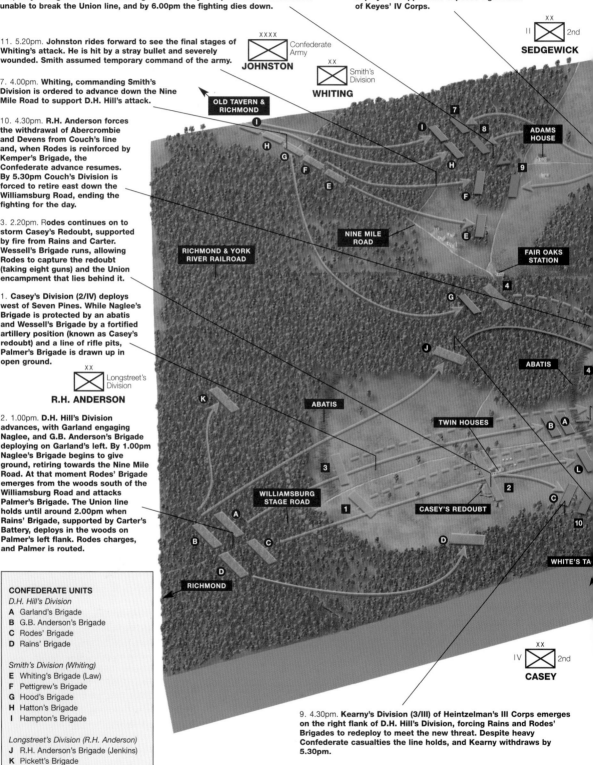

8. 4.30pm. **Sedgwick's leading Brigades deploy in the open ground on either side of the Adams House, supported by artillery. At the same moment the leading Brigades of Whiting's Division reach the area, and realizing the enemy is deployed on their left, they change front to attack Sedgwick's line. By 5.00pm Smith arrives but is unable to break the Union line, and by 6.00pm the fighting dies down.**

11. 5.20pm. **Johnston rides forward to see the final stages of Whiting's attack. He is hit by a stray bullet and severely wounded. Smith assumed temporary command of the army.**

7. 4.00pm. **Whiting, commanding Smith's Division is ordered to advance down the Nine Mile Road to support D.H. Hill's attack.**

10. 4.30pm. **R.H. Anderson forces the withdrawal of Abercrombie and Devens from Couch's line and, when Rodes is reinforced by Kemper's Brigade, the Confederate advance resumes. By 5.30pm Couch's Division is forced to retire east down the Williamsburg Road, ending the fighting for the day.**

3. 2.20pm. **Rodes continues on to storm Casey's Redoubt, supported by fire from Rains and Carter. Wessell's Brigade runs, allowing Rodes to capture the redoubt (taking eight guns) and the Union encampment that lies behind it.**

1. **Casey's Division (2/IV) deploys west of Seven Pines. While Naglee's Brigade is protected by an abatis and Wessell's Brigade by a fortified artillery position (known as Casey's redoubt) and a line of rifle pits, Palmer's Brigade is drawn up in open ground.**

X X
Longstreet's Division
R.H. ANDERSON

2. 1.00pm. **D.H. Hill's Division advances, with Garland engaging Naglee, and G.B. Anderson's Brigade deploying on Garland's left. By 1.00pm Naglee's Brigade begins to give ground, retiring towards the Nine Mile Road. At that moment Rodes' Brigade emerges from the woods south of the Williamsburg Road and attacks Palmer's Brigade. The Union line holds until around 2.00pm when Rains' Brigade, supported by Carter's Battery, deploys in the woods on Palmer's left flank. Rodes charges, and Palmer is routed.**

6. 3.00pm. **Sedgwick's Division (2/II) of Sumner's II Corps reaches the battlefield ahead of the rest of the Corps, and deploys to support the exposed right flank of Keyes' IV Corps.**

XX
II ⊠ 2nd
SEDGEWICK

XXXX
⊠ Confederate Army
JOHNSTON

XX
⊠ Smith's Division
WHITING

OLD TAVERN & RICHMOND

ADAMS HOUSE

NINE MILE ROAD

RICHMOND & YORK RIVER RAILROAD

FAIR OAKS STATION

ABATIS

TWIN HOUSES

ABATIS

WILLIAMSBURG STAGE ROAD

CASEY'S REDOUBT

WHITE'S TA

RICHMOND

XX
IV ⊠ 2nd
CASEY

CONFEDERATE UNITS

D.H. Hill's Division
A Garland's Brigade
B G.B. Anderson's Brigade
C Rodes' Brigade
D Rains' Brigade

Smith's Division (Whiting)
E Whiting's Brigade (Law)
F Pettigrew's Brigade
G Hood's Brigade
H Hatton's Brigade
I Hampton's Brigade

Longstreet's Division (R.H. Anderson)
J R.H. Anderson's Brigade (Jenkins)
K Pickett's Brigade
L Kemper's Brigade

9. 4.30pm. **Kearny's Division (3/III) of Heintzelman's III Corps emerges on the right flank of D.H. Hill's Division, forcing Rains and Rodes' Brigades to redeploy to meet the new threat. Despite heavy Confederate casualties the line holds, and Kearny withdraws by 5.30pm.**

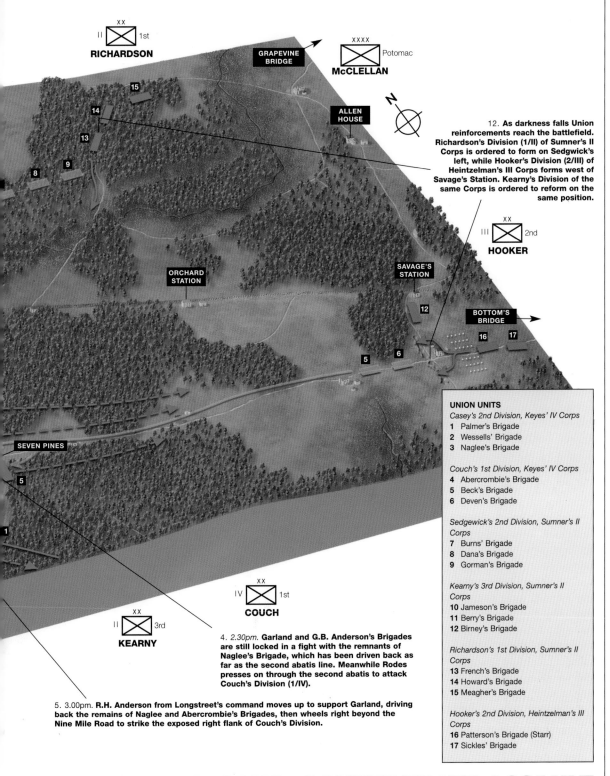

XX
II ☒ 1st
RICHARDSON

GRAPEVINE
BRIDGE

XXXX
☒ Potomac
McCLELLAN

ALLEN
HOUSE

N

15

14

13

9

8

12. **As darkness falls Union reinforcements reach the battlefield. Richardson's Division (1/II) of Sumner's II Corps is ordered to form on Sedgwick's left, while Hooker's Division (2/III) of Heintzelman's III Corps forms west of Savage's Station. Kearny's Division of the same Corps is ordered to reform on the same position.**

XX
III ☒ 2nd
HOOKER

ORCHARD
STATION

SAVAGE'S
STATION

12

BOTTOM'S
BRIDGE

16 17

SEVEN PINES

5

6

5

XX
IV ☒ 1st
COUCH

XX
II ☒ 3rd
KEARNY

4. *2.30pm.* **Garland and G.B. Anderson's Brigades are still locked in a fight with the remnants of Naglee's Brigade, which has been driven back as far as the second abatis line. Meanwhile Rodes presses on through the second abatis to attack Couch's Division (1/IV).**

5. *3.00pm.* **R.H. Anderson from Longstreet's command moves up to support Garland, driving back the remains of Naglee and Abercrombie's Brigades, then wheels right beyond the Nine Mile Road to strike the exposed right flank of Couch's Division.**

UNION UNITS
Casey's 2nd Division, Keyes' IV Corps
1 Palmer's Brigade
2 Wessells' Brigade
3 Naglee's Brigade

Couch's 1st Division, Keyes' IV Corps
4 Abercrombie's Brigade
5 Beck's Brigade
6 Deven's Brigade

Sedgewick's 2nd Division, Sumner's II Corps
7 Burns' Brigade
8 Dana's Brigade
9 Gorman's Brigade

Kearny's 3rd Division, Sumner's II Corps
10 Jameson's Brigade
11 Berry's Brigade
12 Birney's Brigade

Richardson's 1st Division, Sumner's II Corps
13 French's Brigade
14 Howard's Brigade
15 Meagher's Brigade

Hooker's 2nd Division, Heintzelman's III Corps
16 Patterson's Brigade (Starr)
17 Sickles' Brigade

BATTLE OF FAIR OAKS, CONFEDERATE ASSAULT
31 May 1862, viewed from the southwest. In a major attack General Joseph Johnston's Confederate army attempts to destroy those elements of the Army of the Potomac isolated south of the Chickahominy River.

The Allen House, on the Williamsburg Road beside the third line of Union defenses to the west of Savage's Station, was one of several local farmhouses that were turned into temporary casualty stations during and after the battle. (Stratford Archive)

headquarters at 4.00pm that the true extent of the fighting was understood. Johnston immediately ordered Whiting to advance. While this farce was being played out, the Union army was marching to the sound of the guns. Due to some freak of acoustics, the men of Edwin Sumner's II Corps north of the Chickahominy River heard the sounds of battle, while Johnston did not. At 1.30pm, he stood his men to arms, preparing them to intervene in the battle if ordered. An hour later, orders arrived from McClellan, to cross the river and support IV Corps, deploying on the right of Keyes' position. Sumner considered his options. Two crossings were available over the river, at Grapevine Bridge and Lower Bridge, although neither was yet thought capable of supporting troops marching abreast. Sedgwick was duly ordered to lead his division across Grapevine Bridge, while Richardson's men used the Lower Bridge. Union staff officer William Franklin recalled the scene: "*A group of officers with serious, thoughtful countenances and bespattered with mud from head to foot stand discussing as to whether it is safe to trust the troops on so frail and apparently unsafe a structure.*" The bridge held, and the thin columns of Union troops snaked over Grapevine Bridge. Richardson found his crossing too dangerous, and was forced to cross behind Sedgwick. The crossing of 2nd Division took the best part of two hours to complete, but by 4.30pm Gorman's Brigade (1/2/II) of John Sedgwick's Division was approaching the Hanover Road, north of Fair Oaks Station. The guns were lagging behind. A Massachusetts private in the brigade later wrote: "*Most of our artillery became so badly mired that we were obliged to proceed without it.*" As the brigade emerged into the clearing near the Adams House, it saw Confederate troops advancing across their front to the south. These were the men of R.H. Anderson's Brigade, who were attacking Abercrombie's Brigade of Couch's Division, lined up in the woods near Fair Oaks. Gorman formed up his men in the clearing across the Hanover Road, facing south. Burns' Brigade (2/2/II), following on behind, deployed on Gorman's right, while Dana's Brigade (3/2/II) was split into two, with two regiments deploying in the woods on Gorman's left flank while the rest of the brigade formed up between Gorman's and Burns' positions. The artillery of Sedgwick's Division unlimbered in front of the Adams House. The First Division was still on the road from the Upper Bridge, but Sumner ordered Richardson to form up on Sedgwick's left, forming a link between Sedgwick and Couch. By 5.00pm, when Sumner joined Sedgwick near the Adams

House, most of the Second Division was in position, forming a defensive position to the north of Fair Oaks Station. They were just in time.

At that moment the leading troops of Whiting's Division emerged on the edge of the clearing on the Nine Mile Road. Pettigrew's Brigade was in the lead, and the brigade deployed into line facing Gorman. The Carolinian and Georgian troops of Hampton's Brigade filed off into the woods to the north, on Pettigrew's left flank. Hatton's Brigade remained in reserve behind Pettigrew, in the woods on either side of the Nine Mile Road. Then, Whiting gave the order to attack. Pettigrew advanced towards Gorman's line, but the Confederate attack stalled when it was raked by enfilading fire from the Union batteries around the Adams House. A Union soldier recalled: "*Kirby's five Napoleon guns came up, and in the angle of the woods opened with splendid precision upon the Confederate columns. The recoil of the pieces was often so great as to bury the wheels nearly to the hub in the mud.*" Hampton's Brigade veered slightly to the left as it advanced through the woods, meaning that it was unable to form up on the left of Pettigrew's Brigade. It came under fire from both the artillery and the men of Dana's Brigade, and this second Confederate advance also ground to a halt. Even worse, the two brigades began to give ground, withdrawing from the hail of Union fire. Whiting ordered Hatton's Brigade to advance into the gap between his two forward brigades in an attempt to regain the initiative. Meanwhile, Law's Brigade arrived, and Whiting sent it down towards Fair Oaks Station, in an attempt to drive a wedge between the Union forces of Sedgwick and Couch. Finally Hood's Texas Brigade was ordered into the woods south of the Nine Mile Road, where it was supposed to link up with D.H. Hill's left wing. The same Union soldier described what happened next: "*The Confederate lines came dashing upon us with their shrill yells. We received them with a volley from our rifles, and the battery gave them its compliments. The gray masses of the enemy were seen dimly through the smoke, scattering to cover.*" Hatton's men faltered when the brigade commander was killed. On the right, Pettigrew fell, seriously wounded, and the renewed advance finally ground to a complete halt. When Hampton was wounded in the foot, Whiting lost the last of his brigade commanders, and the Confederates began to retreat back into

THE STORMING OF CASEY'S REDOUBT (pages 74–75)

The defensive positions occupied by Brigadier General Casey's men around Fair Oaks and Seven Pines were rudimentary; more of an impediment to an attacker than a serious obstacle. An abatis of felled trees was sited to the west of the Seven Pines clearing, providing some protection for the men of Brigadier General Naglee's Brigade when their positions were attacked on 31 May. When the Union troops were fully engaged, the Confederate brigade of Brigadier General Robert Rodes advanced into the clearing to the south of the abatis, to the right of the Williamsburg Road. Ahead of him lay Casey's Redoubt, an artillery position designed to hold a battery of field pieces. This position was merely a large artillery emplacement, and lacked more elaborate defenses such as a ditch, infantry firing steps or outlying works. A line of rifle pits stretched from the southern edge of the clearing to the redoubt and then beyond to the Williamsburg Road. The skirmish line of Brigadier General Palmer's Brigade held these positions, while the bulk of the brigade was formed up behind the works. Rodes ordered his men to charge across the clearing, an advance hindered by the boggy ground and the clear field of fire in front of the Union positions. The attack faltered, but the arrival of a supporting battery of artillery (Carter's) and the movement of another Confederate infantry brigade (Rains') along the tree line south of the enemy position gave Rodes a second chance to press his attack. He ordered his men to charge again, and within minutes they reached the Union redoubt. The position was held by

artillerymen and a handful of skirmishers (1), as there was insufficient space within the redoubt for both guns and infantry. The defending battery (2) consisted of 12-pdr smoothbore pieces ("Napoleons"), and they managed to inflict heavy casualties on the charging Confederates using both solid shot and canister. This fire proved insufficient to stem the Confederate advance, however, and once the attackers breasted the outworks, the defenders fled. Only small knots of Union gunners and infantrymen stayed behind to fight (3), but within seconds these pockets of resistance were overwhelmed by the tide of Confederate attackers. Brigadier General Rodes (4) was in the forefront of the attack, dismounting in order to join his troops as they stormed the works. He was careful to ensure the attack also overran the rifle pits on either side of the redoubt. The ferocity of the attack was sufficient to break the will of the Union defenders to fight, and the men of Palmer's Brigade joined the artillerymen in a precipitate withdrawal through the Union encampment behind their lines, and eastwards towards the safety of the next Union line. The sodden condition of the ground (5) prevented the gunners of Battery A, 1st New York Light Artillery from removing their pieces, which were all captured. The best account of the action was supplied by Colonel John Brown Gordon (6), a Confederate officer who assumed command of the brigade after Rodes was wounded. He described the heavy casualties inflicted on his Alabama troops during the charge, the wet and muddy terrain the battle was fought in, and the sense of euphoria when the Union position was taken. (Steve Noon)

the woods. By 6.00pm the remains of the three Confederate brigades had completely disengaged, ceding the field to the Union troops. Whiting's attack was a piecemeal affair, and at no time did it seriously threaten Sedgwick. Even worse, two of Whiting's brigades took no part in the fighting. Hood's Brigade spent the late afternoon stumbling through the woods to the south without managing to link up with Hill's troops. Law's men positioned themselves around Fair Oaks, but were never ordered forward to support their comrades. Therefore Whiting missed his opportunity to concentrate his five brigades against Sedgwick's three, and when Richardson's men began to arrive at sunset, the Union line became all but impregnable. Joseph Johnston and Gustavus Smith arrived on the field just as Whiting's men were being driven back for a second time. The Confederate commander sent his deputy back up the Nine Mile Road in search of reinforcements; two brigades from McLaws Division around Old Church were the closest unengaged Confederate troops, but there was no chance these men would arrive on the field before nightfall. It was also a wasted opportunity for the Union, as a counterattack by Sumner against the shattered remains of Whiting's Division would probably have brought about a complete collapse of the Confederate left flank. Instead, Sumner held his men in check, and remained on the defensive. Johnston then rode forward to take a look at the Union line, riding through the Confederate troops milling around in the woods. At that moment he was struck and fell from his horse, severely wounded. He later wrote of the experience: "*About seven o'clock I received a slight wound in the right shoulder from a musket shot, and a few moments after, was unhorsed by a heavy fragment of a shell which struck my breast. Those around had me borne from the field in an ambulance; not however before the President, who was with General Lee not far in the rear, had heard of the accident and visited me, manifesting great concern.*" This left Gustavus Smith in command of the army, and aides raced up the Nine Mile Road to recall him to the front. The trouble was, Johnston had not taken Smith into his confidence and told him his plan of attack. Smith was unsure what was happening to the south, and had no clear idea what to do. As darkness fell, President Jefferson Davis and General Robert E. Lee rode up the Nine Mile Road. The three men watched the closing minutes of the fighting. South of the railroad, Hill's exhausted men withdrew into a reserve position around Casey's Redoubt. They had done all that could be expected of them that day, and more. Longstreet's men held the Confederate front line, facing the Union troops of Kearny and Casey. Behind him, Benjamin Huger's small division reached the Seven Pines crossroads, and Longstreet fed them into the line to the south of the Williamsburg Road while Wilcox, commanding the brigades on Longstreet's left, fought a skirmish in the growing darkness with the Union troops to his front. A Union newspaper reporter recorded his impressions of the dying moments of the battle: "*Darkness … enveloped the fearful spectacle, only to add gloom to its horrors. The enemy still clung in masses to the thick woods, now and then dashing out at a battery, only to be driven back with cruel punishment … There was a fringe of flame blazing on the skirts of the thickets … It was past eight o'clock before the carnage ceased.*" As night fell, Smith ordered Whiting to pull back to the Nine Mile Road to regroup, leaving Hood to bridge the gap between the two Confederate wings. Having command thrust upon him, Smith spent the next few hours trying to figure out what to do with his army. Davis and

One-armed Brigadier General Philip Kearny (commanding 3rd Division of III Corps) helped stabilize the Union line on the Williamsburg Road during the afternoon of 31 May. When he heard that Brigadier General Oliver O. Howard (commanding 1/1/II) lost an arm during the fighting around Fair Oaks, he consoled the invalid, saying, "General, I'm sorry for you, but you must not mind it; the ladies will not think the less of you." (National Archives)

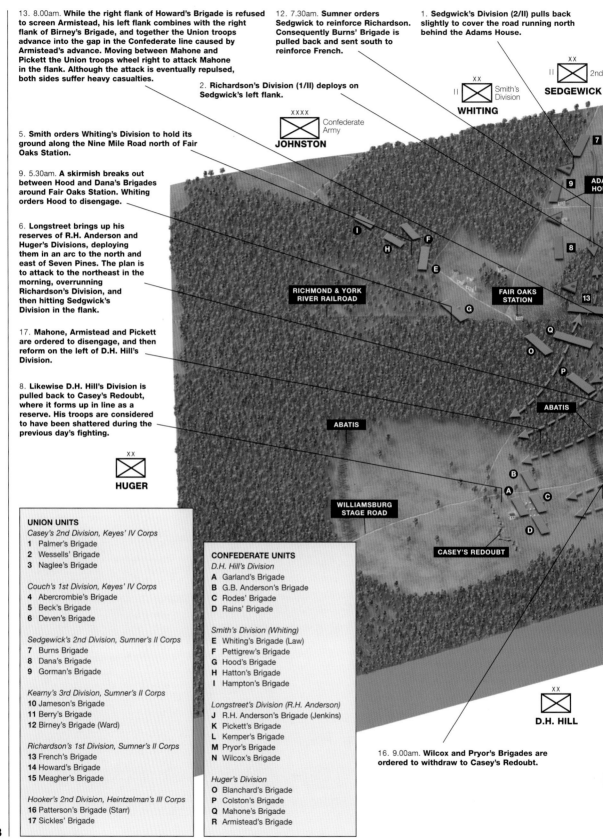

13. 8.00am. While the right flank of Howard's Brigade is refused to screen Armistead, his left flank combines with the right flank of Birney's Brigade, and together the Union troops advance into the gap in the Confederate line caused by Armistead's advance. Moving between Mahone and Pickett the Union troops wheel right to attack Mahone in the flank. Although the attack is eventually repulsed, both sides suffer heavy casualties.

12. 7.30am. Sumner orders Sedgwick to reinforce Richardson. Consequently Burns' Brigade is pulled back and sent south to reinforce French.

1. Sedgwick's Division (2/II) pulls back slightly to cover the road running north behind the Adams House.

2. Richardson's Division (1/II) deploys on Sedgwick's left flank.

5. Smith orders Whiting's Division to hold its ground along the Nine Mile Road north of Fair Oaks Station.

9. 5.30am. A skirmish breaks out between Hood and Dana's Brigades around Fair Oaks Station. Whiting orders Hood to disengage.

6. Longstreet brings up his reserves of R.H. Anderson and Huger's Divisions, deploying them in an arc to the north and east of Seven Pines. The plan is to attack to the northeast in the morning, overrunning Richardson's Division, and then hitting Sedgwick's Division in the flank.

17. Mahone, Armistead and Pickett are ordered to disengage, and then reform on the left of D.H. Hill's Division.

8. Likewise D.H. Hill's Division is pulled back to Casey's Redoubt, where it forms up in line as a reserve. His troops are considered to have been shattered during the previous day's fighting.

16. 9.00am. Wilcox and Pryor's Brigades are ordered to withdraw to Casey's Redoubt.

II ⊠ 2nd — SEDGEWICK

II ⊠ Smith's Division — WHITING

XXXX ⊠ Confederate Army — JOHNSTON

XX ⊠ HUGER

XX ⊠ D.H. HILL

RICHMOND & YORK RIVER RAILROAD

FAIR OAKS STATION

ADAMS HOU

ABATIS

ABATIS

ABATIS

WILLIAMSBURG STAGE ROAD

CASEY'S REDOUBT

UNION UNITS

Casey's 2nd Division, Keyes' IV Corps
1 Palmer's Brigade
2 Wessells' Brigade
3 Naglee's Brigade

Couch's 1st Division, Keyes' IV Corps
4 Abercrombie's Brigade
5 Beck's Brigade
6 Deven's Brigade

Sedgewick's 2nd Division, Sumner's II Corps
7 Burns Brigade
8 Dana's Brigade
9 Gorman's Brigade

Kearny's 3rd Division, Sumner's II Corps
10 Jameson's Brigade
11 Berry's Brigade
12 Birney's Brigade (Ward)

Richardson's 1st Division, Sumner's II Corps
13 French's Brigade
14 Howard's Brigade
15 Meagher's Brigade

Hooker's 2nd Division, Heintzelman's III Corps
16 Patterson's Brigade (Starr)
17 Sickles' Brigade

CONFEDERATE UNITS

D.H. Hill's Division
A Garland's Brigade
B G.B. Anderson's Brigade
C Rodes' Brigade
D Rains' Brigade

Smith's Division (Whiting)
E Whiting's Brigade (Law)
F Pettigrew's Brigade
G Hood's Brigade
H Hatton's Brigade
I Hampton's Brigade

Longstreet's Division (R.H. Anderson)
J R.H. Anderson's Brigade (Jenkins)
K Pickett's Brigade
L Kemper's Brigade
M Pryor's Brigade
N Wilcox's Brigade

Huger's Division
O Blanchard's Brigade
P Colston's Brigade
Q Mahone's Brigade
R Armistead's Brigade

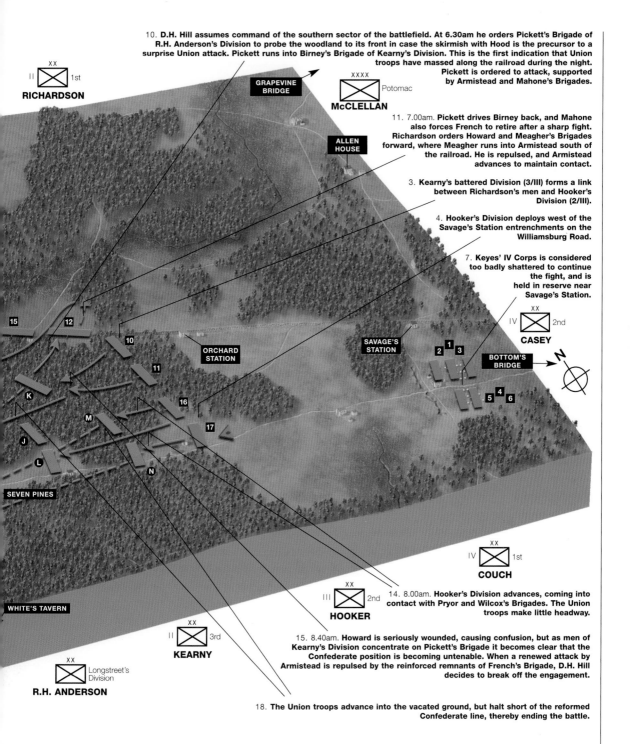

10. D.H. Hill assumes command of the southern sector of the battlefield. At 6.30am he orders Pickett's Brigade of R.H. Anderson's Division to probe the woodland to its front in case the skirmish with Hood is the precursor to a surprise Union attack. Pickett runs into Birney's Brigade of Kearny's Division. This is the first indication that Union troops have massed along the railroad during the night. Pickett is ordered to attack, supported by Armistead and Mahone's Brigades.

11. 7.00am. Pickett drives Birney back, and Mahone also forces French to retire after a sharp fight. Richardson orders Howard and Meagher's Brigades forward, where Meagher runs into Armistead south of the railroad. He is repulsed, and Armistead advances to maintain contact.

3. Kearny's battered Division (3/III) forms a link between Richardson's men and Hooker's Division (2/III).

4. Hooker's Division deploys west of the Savage's Station entrenchments on the Williamsburg Road.

7. Keyes' IV Corps is considered too badly shattered to continue the fight, and is held in reserve near Savage's Station.

14. 8.00am. Hooker's Division advances, coming into contact with Pryor and Wilcox's Brigades. The Union troops make little headway.

15. 8.40am. Howard is seriously wounded, causing confusion, but as men of Kearny's Division concentrate on Pickett's Brigade it becomes clear that the Confederate position is becoming untenable. When a renewed attack by Armistead is repulsed by the reinforced remnants of French's Brigade, D.H. Hill decides to break off the engagement.

18. The Union troops advance into the vacated ground, but halt short of the reformed Confederate line, thereby ending the battle.

Map labels:
II 1st **RICHARDSON**
XXXX Potomac **McCLELLAN**
GRAPEVINE BRIDGE
ALLEN HOUSE
ORCHARD STATION
SAVAGE'S STATION
BOTTOM'S BRIDGE
IV 2nd **CASEY**
IV 1st **COUCH**
III 2nd **HOOKER**
II 3rd **KEARNY**
Longstreet's Division **R.H. ANDERSON**
SEVEN PINES
WHITE'S TAVERN

BATTLE OF FAIR OAKS, UNION COUNTERATTACK

1 June 1862, viewed from the southwest. The Confederates renew their attacks but they are beaten off by the reinforced and reorganized Union troops. The Confederates withdraw to a new line around Seven Pines.

Lee returned to Richmond, and the President ordered Lee to assume command of the army. Both men were unaware of Johnston's plan, so Lee decided to let Smith continue in command until the battle was decided. Night had brought the fighting to a close, but both sides knew that the battle would almost certainly continue the following morning. Both Smith and McClellan tried to bring some order to the chaos, and to concoct a plan that would salvage victory from confusion.

A correspondent from the *Richmond Dispatch* recalled the scene that evening behind the Confederate lines. "*What pen can describe the scene presented on every side? Friend and foe scattered far and wide in death or in last agonies. Here and there are deserted camps; dead and dying fill the tents. Horses wounded and lame rush to and fro. Here are artillerymen, some Federals, some Confederate, wounded or dead, within a few feet of each other. Every wound known to the human body is seen in ghastly reality. All crave water, and, crawling through the mud, lap the bloodstained and slimy flood. Some curse, some moan, and turn their eyes towards heaven sadly. Rebels hand out water to their late foes, and eyes glisten in thankfullness. Squads of prisoners are seen issuing from the woods in divers places, and scowl upon their captors ominously, while others whistle and joke along the road as if infinitely gratified at being captured. Here comes a stalwart Alabamian, left hand shattered and in a sling, carrying off triumphantly the colors of the 5th Pennsylvania Volunteers, keeping a watchful eye on the* [captured] *standard bearer by his side.*" The scene in the Union camp was equally grim. Chaplain Marks helping the surgeons at Savage's Station wrote: "*During the entire night the wounded were brought in until they covered the grounds around the house of Mr. Savage, and filled all the outhouses, barns and sheds ... All night the surgeons were occupied in amputations ... One spectacle of anguish and agony only succeeded another. The mind was overwhelmed and benumbed by such scenes of accumulated misery.*"

During the night the unwounded Union troops remained busy. Richardson's Division formed up along the Richmond & York River Railroad, extending to the southeast from Sedgwick's left flank along the Hanover Road. Sedgwick himself had pulled his men back slightly, to create a better defensive line. Richardson's left linked up with

On 1 June, Union troops of Brigadier General Thomas F. Meagher's Brigade (2/1/II) managed to stave off the rout of William H. French's Brigade (3/1/II) near Fair Oaks Station by counterattacking southwards across the Richmond & York River Railroad. In this depiction of the battle, men of the 69th and 88th New York Volunteers advance towards the woods in the distance, held by Virginia troops commanded by Brigadier General Lewis A. Armistead. (Virginia War Museum)

Birney's Brigade of Kearny's Division, which formed the right flank of Heintzelman's III Corps. Hooker's Division took up position on the Union left astride the Williamsburg Road, while the shattered remnants of Keyes' IV Corps were pulled back into reserve around Savage's Station. This meant that when dawn broke, the Union troops presented an unbroken line, snaking south from the Adams House to the third line of defenses on the Williamsburg Road. For their part, the Confederate troops remained where they were. It was all Smith could do to figure out where his troops were, and any further marshalling was impossible. Smith had no clear idea of what had happened to Longstreet to the south, and had lost contact with Huger. During the night word gradually filtered north. J.E.B. Stuart reported that the Charles City Road was devoid of Union defenders, and that Huger's men had never appeared. Then, Longstreet reported that his assault the previous day had met with moderate success, and that the first two Union lines had fallen to D.H. Hill's assault. In order to build up a clearer picture, Smith ordered Longstreet to report to the army headquarters for a meeting. At 1.00am the two commanders met, and together they devised a plan for a renewed attack the following morning. Whiting's Division would act as the anvil to Longstreet's hammer. Whiting would form a line across the Nine Mile Road facing Sedgwick. Longstreet would screen Hooker's troops with two brigades commanded by Wilcox (those of Wilcox and Pryor), R.H. Anderson with Jenkins' Brigade remained in reserve, ready to exploit any success or plug a gap in the line as Longstreet advanced. Kemper's Brigade was considered too spent to continue the action. Longstreet's remaining brigades (Pickett and Colston) would swing north to hit Sedgwick in the flank, supported by two of Huger's brigades (Armistead and Mahone). To the north, McLaws was ordered to ready his troops to face a Union counterattack across the Chickahominy River, or to support Whiting if the latter was attacked. In theory, this sounded like a good plan. In reality, the brigades of Huger and Longstreet were intermingled in the woods to the north and east of Seven Pines, and the coordination of any attack was all but impossible.

Sedgwick's men were in a good position. Dana's Brigade was on the left, anchored on the railroad. Gorman's Brigade was deployed to its right, lined up behind the Hanover Road facing the woods occupied by Whiting's Confederates. Burns formed up to the north, marking the right flank of the Union line. Sedgwick's artillery was dispersed along the line in support of the infantry. Richardson's Division was formed up behind Dana's Brigade, with its front on the railroad, facing south. Only French's Brigade (3/1/II) was up front, formed up at right angles to Dana's left flank. Behind French was Howard's Brigade, while Meagher's 2nd Brigade was deployed behind French's left flank. Richardson's artillery was concentrated at the apex of the Union line, between Dana and French. This was exactly the point where Longstreet intended to direct his attack. Then came Kearny' Division; three brigades, forming a link between Hooker and Richardson in the woods between the railroad and the Williamsburg Road. Keyes' troops could not be expected to fight that morning after their rough handling the previous day. Likewise, Jameson's and Berry's brigades of Kearny's Division were too shattered to take part in the fighting.

Longstreet had helped plan the assault, but for some reason he elected to let Daniel Hill carry it out. He rode off, after saying to Hill: *"You have here taken the bull by the horns, and must fight him out."* Longstreet never gave Hill clear instructions, and although he had 13 brigades at his disposal, Hill was only given control over the four earmarked to lead the assault in addition to his own four shattered brigades, which were ordered to remain in reserve. It was another wasted opportunity. The battle began shortly after dawn (around 6.00am) when Hood's Brigade probed forward around Fair Oaks Station, and clashed with Dana's Brigade. Whiting was reluctant to risk his most powerful brigade in a piecemeal attack, and he reined Hood in. From that point on, D.H. Hill's men were on their own. The battle proper began around 6.30am, when Hill ordered Pickett to advance into the woods to his front in an attempt to pin any Union troops they encountered. At that point Hill had no idea that Richardson's and Kearny's divisions lay in his way, and he imagined that Sedgwick and Hooker were alone on the field. Pickett's men ran into Birney's Brigade to the south of the railroad, and soon the two sides were locked in a firefight. Hill ordered up

Union army surgeons worked throughout the night of 31 May as the wounded were brought back to their casualty stations for medical attention. Although conditions were primitive, the Army of the Potomac enjoyed a far superior medical arm than the Confederates. (Stratford Archive)

Armistead's and Mahone's brigades in support, ordering them to advance on Pickett's left flank. He also requested Pickett to join in the general advance, as he still imagined he was only facing a light screen of enemy troops. Within minutes Mahone came into contact with the left wing of French's Brigade, and managed to drive them back in disorder. Sumner realized that the Confederates were about to drive a wedge between his two divisions, so he ordered Sedgwick to redeploy Burns' Brigade, pulling it out of its position on the Hanover Road and sending it south to reinforce French. At the same time, Richardson ordered his two unengaged brigades forward. The fight between Pickett and Birney saw the Union brigade give ground, drawing Pickett's men off to the right. This created a gap in the Confederate line immediately in front of Richardson's left wing. Armistead's Brigade was moving forward to plug this gap, but its advance led to it meeting Howard's Brigade in the woods by the railroad. By 8.00am French's men were in full retreat, but Mahone and Armistead became entangled with Howard's right, so the Confederates failed to slam into the flank of Sedgwick's line. The two sides were now hopelessly entangled, and units had little idea where their front lay. Confederate Colonel Tomlin recalled, "*that friends and enemies were so indiscriminately mixed up together* [that there was] *more danger from friends than from the enemy.*" The two regiments on Howard's flank made contact with the right wing of Birney's Brigade, and this ad hoc force pressed forward, finding a gap between Armistead and Pickett. The Virginians held their ground, repulsing the Union attack. Indeed, Pickett reported to Hill that if he would "*send more troops and some ammunition to me we would drive the enemy across the Chickahominy.*" In reality, Pickett was outnumbered, and isolated deep in the woods. Pickett might have continued to hold his ground, but elsewhere the Confederates were beginning to fall back. According to a Union witness, Armistead's men had attacked three times, but then broke. Just as the battle was swinging in favor of the Union, General Howard was wounded. Within minutes the Union troops in his vicinity withdrew to the railroad, just as Burns' Brigade moved into position to relieve French. On the left, as Mahone's men began to waver and break, D.H. Hill rode up, and accused them of being cowards. The brigadier

extorted: "*You should not abuse my men, for I ordered them out of the fight.*" Hill then rounded on Mahone, and accused him of disobeying orders. "Little Billy" Mahone "*fairly foamed*", and took the rebuke so personally that he considered challenging his superior to a duel. The moment passed, but it was becoming clear that the Confederate attack was not going to succeed.

The fighting along the railroad fizzled out by 8.30am, but further to the east Wilcox was coming under pressure. Hooker had ordered his men to advance into contact to their front at 7.00am, initiating a bloody skirmish in the woods. Chaplain Marks later wrote: "*Our men were in line of battle about 100 yards in advance of this house* [Savage's Station]*, in the edge of the forest. It was now about 7am. The firing was very brisk and steady all along our front lines, but having none of the regularity and continuous roar of battle, but lively skirmishing.*" Wilcox and Pryor held their ground, but when Pickett's Brigade was pulled back from its exposed position, Hill decided to call an end to the attack. It was clear the Confederate assault was going nowhere. He ordered Wilcox and Pryor to fall back towards Seven Pines, supported by R.H. Anderson. Similarly the brigades of Pickett, Armistead, and Mahone were ordered to fall back and form a new defensive line to the west. The Union troops advanced cautiously, but when they saw the strength of the Confederate position around Seven Pines they halted under cover of the woods, bringing an end to the day's fighting.

The battle of Fair Oaks was over, but neither side really knew it. Neither side was willing to repeat the chaos of the previous 24 hours. It was almost as if the battle ended by mutual consent, as the two dazed combatants took stock. Johnston's offensive had come to naught, and seemingly achieved nothing apart from a high butcher's bill of over 11,000 men, and the loss of the Confederate commander. Few present could have appreciated quite how far-reaching the effects of the battle were to be.

AFTERMATH

During 2 June, both sides watched each other warily, as neither Lee nor McClellan was willing to resume the fight. For the Confederates, their surprise attack had failed, and it was clear that the Union army south of the river would now be heavily reinforced. For his part, McClellan's army had suffered serious losses, largely due to their commander's poor dispositions. This fact would prey on "Little Mac" during the coming weeks, and the action strengthened his belief that he was heavily outnumbered by the Confederates. Why else would a defensively minded commander like Johnston risk an all-out attack?

Late in the afternoon of 2 June, Hooker's Division (2/III) probed the Confederate positions around Seven Pines. He discovered that Longstreet and D.H. Hill had withdrawn their respective divisions back towards Richmond, and the Confederate line was held by the relatively fresh men of Huger's Division. Unable to determine the true extent of the Confederate defenses, Hooker decided not to press his attack, and withdrew to the east. North of the railroad, Whiting's battered division remained in place astride the Nine Mile Road. On the Union side, Sumner's II Corps remained south of the Chickahominy River, while McClellan's remaining two Corps waited in vain for McDowell.

Naturally, McClellan claimed that the battle was a defensive victory, although privately he was distressed by the loss of life. With an equal lack of conviction, the Richmond press proclaimed the battle to be a victory. Certainly the cost had been high for such an inconclusive battle. The Confederate losses over the two-day battle at Fair Oaks totaled 6,134 men (980 killed, 4,749 wounded and 405 missing); some 10 per cent of the entire army. Union losses amounted to 5,032 men (790 killed, 3,594 wounded, and 647 missing); some 5 per cent of the Army of the Potomac. The Union wounded were brought to Savage's Station, while the Confederates were transported into Richmond for treatment. The number of casualties overwhelmed the primitive medical facilities of both armies, but a flock of volunteers on both sides did what they could to ease the suffering. Eventually, the Union casualties were taken to White House landing, where hospital ships were provided for them. The injured Confederates were taken into the homes of the people of Richmond, where the genteel ladies of the city played their part in tending their wounds. Meanwhile, the newspapers of both sides printed the long list of casualties, and the politicians and citizens girded themselves for the next round of bloody conflict. The battle had decided nothing, save that the war would be longer and bloodier than anyone had thought.

The most significant outcome of the battle was the loss of Joseph E. Johnston as commander of the Confederate army, and his replacement during the evening of 1 June by Robert E. Lee. McClellan greeted the

CONFEDERATE CAVALRY LOOT TUNSTALL'S STATION DURING STUART'S "RIDE AROUND MCCLELLAN"

(pages 86–87)

Following the carnage at Fair Oaks (31 May–1 June 1862), General Robert E. Lee assumed command of the Confederate Army, which was renamed the Army of Northern Virginia. While McClellan's Army of the Potomac remained in its position astride the Chickahominy River, Lee began to plan a Confederate counter-offensive, an operation that would go down in history as "the Seven Days Campaign". Lee's strategy involved turning the flank of the Union troops north of the river, then driving them back until he cut their lines of supply. Before that happened, he needed to know how far north the Union flank extended. He therefore ordered his cavalry commander, Brigadier General James Ewell Brown Stuart to lead a reconnaissance to probe around the northern flank of the Union army. Stuart, the consummate cavalier was delighted with the mission, and led his men in a wide sweep from Hanover Court House to the Pamunkey River, where he discovered that the Union right flank did not extend much beyond its main encampments along the Chickahominy River. After driving Union cavalry patrols back he reached Tunstall's Station, on the Richmond & York River Railroad. This was McClellan's main supply line, and Stuart's troopers found themselves amidst huge stockpiles of ammunition, provisions and other supplies. The attack caught the Union army by surprise, and only a handful of rear-echelon troops were in the area. In this scene, J.E.B. Stuart is shown conferring with

his staff (1), while his troopers pillage a Union wagon train filled with supplies. The Union soldiers at Tunstall's Station offered little or no resistance (2), as they seemed stunned by the sudden arrival of the Confederate horsemen. Hundreds of prisoners were rounded up (3) and the majority of these were spirited away through Union lines to Richmond, where they were duly imprisoned. The Confederate troopers filled their saddlebags with food (4), although the abstemious Stuart forbade the drinking of looted alcohol during the mission. Union cavalry remounts and other horses were also taken by Stuart's men (5), while other less portable items such as ammunition and clothing were burned in a conflagration that lasted for days. In the middle of all this, a Union supply train appeared and, despite Confederate attempts to block the tracks, it refused to stop (6). Instead the engineer increased speed, crashing through a barrier placed across the tracks. The Confederate troopers fired on the train as it sped past, killing the engineer, but it suffered little damage and escaped to raise the alarm. This prompted Stuart to gather his men and withdraw, before the Union army could arrive in force to trap him behind enemy lines. Instead of returning the way he had come, Stuart chose to head south, crossing the James River, then leading his men west along the Charles City Road towards the safety of Richmond. The "Ride around McClellan" raised Confederate morale, humiliated McClellan and provided Lee with the military information he so badly needed, all for the loss of only one man. (Steve Noon)

During J.E.B. Stuart's ride around McClellan's army, the only serious engagement was fought to the west of Old Church, during the early afternoon of Friday, 13 June. During a brief mounted skirmish, Captain Latané of the 9th Virginia Cavalry was killed by his counterpart Captain Royall of the US 5th Cavalry. Despite this personal victory, the Union troopers were routed. (Stratford Archive)

news with glee, as he considered Lee to be a less capable and far less aggressive commander than Johnston. He was proved wrong. On 2 June, Lee finally assumed formal command of the army, establishing his headquarters outside the Widow Dabbs House on the Nine Mile Road, a mile and a half from Richmond. Even his own men had little faith in their new commander, dubbing him the "King of Spades" for his orders to dig in between Seven Pines and Richmond. The new commander also brought with him a new name for his army. From the moment Lee assumed command, the army became known as the Army of Northern Virginia. Lee did not intend to remain fighting with his capital to his back. He would defeat McClellan, then take the fight north to reclaim the lost soil of Virginia.

While McClellan continued to plan the final stage of his advance on Richmond, relying on artillery to blast his way through the Confederate defenses, Lee was developing his own plans. First, he had to determine the exact disposition of McClellan's army. Consequently, on 10 June, he met his cavalry commander, the flamboyant J.E.B. Stuart. Days before, Stuart had written that, "*with profound personal regard for General Lee, he has disappointed me as a general.*" He would soon change his opinion. Lee explained that he was planning an attack, and needed to know where the Union right wing ended. Stuart was the ideal man for the mission. On 12 June, he rode north from Richmond at the head of 1,200 troopers. After spending the night in bivouac some 22 miles north of the city, he turned east, probing with Union patrols around Hanover Court House, then cutting past them to the southeast. A Union force of mounted and dismounted cavalry barred his way at a crossing over the Totopotomoy Creek, but a spirited charge up the ravine-lined approach road dispersed the enemy, and the advance continued. The pursuit continued to Old Church, a little over two miles beyond the creek, where another mounted charge broke the next line of Union cavalry. The Union camp at Old Church was put to the torch, while civilians brought food and drink out to their Confederate liberators. Aware that the Union army would be in pursuit, Stuart decided that a return through Hanover would be impossible. Instead, he took the momentous decision to ride clear around the Union army, returning to Richmond along the James River.

The raid continued. The Confederate horsemen moved out towards Tunstall's Station, a halt on the Richmond & York River Railroad. The railroad station was captured after a brief fight, and Stuart's men found themselves the owners of supply wagons, stockpiles of food, and a growing band of prisoners. Looting what they could, the rest of the wagons were burned. At that moment a Union supply train appeared from the east, but when its driver found the station in enemy hands he increased speed. The train ran the gauntlet of Confederate carbine fire as it sped past. Stuart took the precaution of destroying a railroad bridge to prevent the inevitable Union response. He then led his men south,

marching through the night until the force reached the Chickahominy River. The river was in spate, forcing Stuart's men to spend valuable hours building a temporary bridge. Somehow the whole force crossed the river before the Union troops arrived on the north bank. With the bridge blown behind them, the road was now relatively clear. From Charles City Court House the troopers rode west along the James River until they reached the safety of the Confederate lines outside Richmond. An exhausted Stuart finally rode into Lee's headquarters at dawn on 15 June, some 48 hours after he left. Only one Confederate was killed during the whole operation.

J.E.B. Stuart's ride around McClellan had humiliated the Union commander and his men and proved a great morale boost for the Confederates. Even more importantly, Stuart's ride had provided Lee with the information he needed to finalize plans for his attack; an offensive that would become known as the Seven Days. The result would be the defeat of McClellan, the retreat of his army from the peninsula, and the sparing of Richmond from the invader. This was made possible by the sacrifices made at Fair Oaks. If Johnston had been unable to surprise McClellan, the Union commander would have continued his advance on the Confederate capital. The battle marked a turning point, as from that moment on, McClellan lost his nerve. After Fair Oaks, the initiative in the Eastern Theater would pass to the Confederates. Under the leadership of Robert E. Lee, the Army of Northern Virginia would inflict the first of a series of humiliating defeats on the Army of the Potomac within miles of the Fair Oaks battlefield. These hard-won Confederate victories would ensure that Richmond remained safe from attack for three more years, until the final collapse of the Confederate cause in the spring of 1865. It also meant that the bloodletting would continue.

THE BATTLEFIELD TODAY

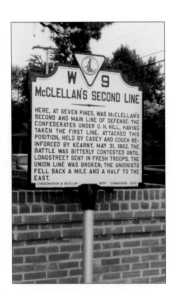

The location of the second line of Union defense east of Seven Pines is denoted by this Virginia State Marker, located at the junction of the Nine Mile and Williamsburg roads. (Author's photograph)

In July 1944, the Richmond National Battlefield Park was established by act of Congress. The park consisted of several areas of importance to the history of the Peninsula Campaign that had been acquired through private donation to the Commonwealth of Virginia in 1932. Today the National Parks Service, a Federal agency run by the US Department of the Interior, administers the Richmond National Battlefield Park. It consists of nearly 800 acres of land in ten sites throughout the area, and boasts a number of superb museums and interpretation centers both on the sites themselves and in Richmond. The main visitor center is located on the site of the Tredegar Iron Works on the banks of the James River in downtown Richmond, while a major satellite is located in Chimborazo Park on the eastern outskirts of the city. From this base, visitors can embark on a tour of the park's sites: a 57-mile trail sign-posted by markers, maps, and interpretative panels. The ten sites include battlefields, permanent batteries, field fortifications, and historic buildings, and the visitor really needs at least two days to fully explore all these locations. While the site of the battle of Fair Oaks is not included in the Battlefield Park, the tour permits visitors to trace the entire history of the Peninsula Campaign. Another National Park Service site at Yorktown and a series of interpretative markers around Williamsburg, Fair Oaks, and elsewhere in the Peninsula allow visitors to walk the ground of the early stages of the Peninsula Campaign.

Fort Monroe is now part of the urban sprawl on the southeastern tip of the Tidewater Peninsula that encompasses Newport News and Hampton. The casemate museum within the fort is well worth a visit, and the displays include the rooms used by General McClellan as his first headquarters during the campaign. The Virginia Military Museum in Newport News is also worth a detour, and contains artifacts relating to the campaign. Further up the peninsula at Yorktown, the site of General Magruder's defensive works forms part of the Colonial National Historical Park, run by the National Park Service. Although the interpretative emphasis is on the Revolutionary War, a visit to the earthworks will reveal the imposing nature of the town's defenses in 1862. The Yorktown National Cemetery on the edge of the Battlefield Park contains the graves of some 2,200 casualties of the Civil War campaigns in the region. Magruder's line followed Beaverdam Creek, a tributary of the Warwick River. An indication of the physical barrier this flooded creek posed to the advancing Union army can be gained by a visit to the Newport News Reservoir, where I-64 crosses the creek along a dam, built on the site of one of Magruder's defended crossing points.

At Williamsburg little remains of the Civil War defenses to the east of the town, although markers on US Route 60 and Quarterpath Road indicate the position of part of the Confederate defensive line. Just over

The Hanover Road merged with the Nine Mile Road at the railroad crossing a few yards west of Fair Oaks Station. In this view, looking east along the railroad from the Nine Mile Road crossing, the station would have been located on the left of the photograph. The main fighting on 1 June took place along this railroad track. (Author's photograph)

nine miles from Yorktown on the Colonial Parkway and some two miles from Williamsburg is Jones Mill Pond, where the remains of a Confederate trench network can still be seen. This is one of three remaining parts of the Williamsburg lines, and is the site of the outflanking maneuver by Hancock's Division that gave the attackers a foothold in the Confederate defensive line. The interstate highway at this part of the battlefield runs northwest to southeast and the point at which it crosses the colonial Parkway marks the sight of Early's clash with Hancock. The ambitious visitor can walk the ground of this part of the battlefield, which is now bisected by I-64. To the south of the interstate, part of Fort Magruder is preserved close to the aptly named Magruder Elementary School. The southern portion of the Confederate line was anchored on Tutter's Neck Pond, which still exists a half mile to the southwest of the marker on US Route 60. The Confederate troops who counterattacked during the late morning began the battle in the area now occupied by the Golden Horseshoe Green Course, the axis of advance taking them across US Route 60 in the vicinity of the hotel and restaurant complex to the east of the battlefield marker (where a part of the Confederate lines can still be seen). Hooker's troops attacked Fort Magruder from just north of what is now the junction of Route 60 and the Williamsburg Bypass Road (State Route 199), the furthest point of advance being marked by the modern site of the Magruder Middle School. Colonial Williamsburg itself contains several buildings that were occupied by enemy troops after the battle, and detailed information on these historic sites can be obtained from the Visitor Center.

Turning to the Fair Oaks battlefield, although no parcel of land was saved for posterity, several key features of the battlefield still remain in and around the Richmond suburb of Sandston. First, the principal roads that played such an important part in the battle still exist. The Williamsburg Stage Road (now called the Williamsburg Road, or US Route 60) follows the same course it did in late May 1862, as does Nine Mile Road (State Route 33), which bisects it at Seven Pines National Cemetery. The Richmond & York River Railroad is marked by an extant railroad line (now the Southern Railroad) immediately to the north of I-64, which follows the path of the old railroad through Fair Oaks. Its modern junction with Airport Drive is located just over a half mile to the east of the Fair Oaks junction, and visitors using the Interstate will have to use this road to join the two major arteries crossing the 1862 battlefield. The Cemetery is located on the northeast corner of the Nine Mile Road and Williamsburg Road junction, and marks the location of the third line of Union defenses, a position occupied by Abercrombie's Brigade of Couch's Division during the battle. The line of the abatis immediately to the west of the Seven Oaks junction follows the line of Eastland Drive, a small residential street leading onto US Route 60 from the north. The twin houses no longer exist, but their location can be determined in relation to the Seven Pines junction to the east, somewhere in the lot south of the road, at the end of Taraby Place, part of the network of small roads to the south of US Route 60. Slightly further to the east is Casey Street, marking the location of Casey's Redoubt during the battle. A library marks the location of the line of rifle pits occupied by Wessells' Brigade. The ground occupied by Naglee's Brigade of Casey's Division is harder to find, but if we assume that the first abatis line was laid along what is now Jackson Avenue, then we can assume the first line of Union defenders occupied the line of the modern Confederate Avenue. If we assume Rodes' Brigade attacked to the south of the Williamsburg Stage Road, then its line of advance crossed the northern fringes of what is now Richmond International Airport (Byrd Field).

Further to the north, R.H. Anderson's attack on the north of the Union position around Seven Pines would have crossed the Nine Mile Road roughly where Garland Avenue joins the road today, then smashed into Abercrombie's position close to where Dakar Drive and Seven Pines Avenue are today. While it is unfortunate little remains of the battlefield apart from markers erected by the Richmond National Battlefield Park and by the State, the road network still allows us to gain some impression of the spatial relationship of the Union lines of defense.

Around Fair Oaks the road used by Sedgwick's Division of Sumner's Corps to reach Fair Oaks follows the modern Hanover Road. The ground covered by Whiting's attack against this hastily formed Union line can be traced by following Hart Street and Cedarwood Road immediately before the Hanover and Nine Mile junction. The open space crossed by Whiting's men is now occupied by residential housing (an area now known as Fairlawn Heights), so it is hard to gain any impression of the terrain as it appeared in 1862. The ground occupied by Richardson's Division on the second day of the battle conforms to the line of Defense Avenue, a residential cul-de-sac to the south of I-64 that can be accessed from Dakar Drive. By following Hanover Road and Airport Drive (State Route 156) you reach the Chickahominy River in the vicinity of Grapevine Bridge, the crucial link between McClellan's forces, and the route taken by Sumner's Corps as it marched to the sound of the guns.

Finally, visitors to the Richmond area have to visit the Museum of the Confederacy, on the corner of East Clay and 12th Street in the center of the city. Amongst its exhibits are displays on the Peninsula Campaign, and the uniforms worn by General Johnston and Brigadier General J.E.B. Stuart. Although a superb museum, the exhibits cover the whole sweep of the war. For a more detailed explanation of the Peninsula Campaign the Tredegar headquarters of the Richmond National Battlefield Park on Tredegar Street is the place to go.

BIBLIOGRAPHY

Bailey, Ronald H., and the editors of Time-Life Books, *Forward to Richmond: McClellan's Peninsular Campaign* (Alexandria, VA, 1984)

Bridges, Hal, *Lee's Maverick General: Daniel Harvey Hill* (New York, NY, 1961)

Burton, Brian K., *Extraordinary Circumstances: The Seven Days Battles* (Boomington, IN, 2001)

Catton, Bruce, *Mr. Lincoln's Army* (New York, NY, 1952)

Current, Richard N., *Encyclopaedia of the Confederacy* (New York, NY, 1993). Four volumes

Dowdey, Clifford, *Lee Takes Command* (New York, NY, 1964). (First published as *The Seven Days: The emergence of Lee*)

Esposito, Colonel Vincent J., *West Point Atlas of American Wars* (New York, NY, 1959). Two volumes. Volume 1 is pertinent to the campaign

Evans, Clement A. (ed.), *Confederate Military History* (Atlanta, GA, 1899). Twelve volumes

Foote, Shelby, *The Civil War: A Narrative* (New York, NY, 1958). 3 volumes.

Freeman, D.S., *Lee's Lieutenants: A Study in Command* (New York, NY, 1943). Two volumes

Hassler, Warren W., *General George B. McClellan* (Baton Rouge, LA, 1957)

Heitman, Francis B., *Biographical Register and Dictionary of the United States Army, 1789–1903* (Washington, D.C., 1903). Two volumes. Reprinted by the University of Illinois Press (Urbana, IL, 1965)

Hubbell, John T., and Geary, James W., *Biographical Dictionary of the Union: Northern Leaders of the Civil War* (Westport, CT, 1995)

Hudson, Carson O., Jr., *Civil War Williamsburg* (Mechanicsburg, PA, 1997)

Katcher, Philip, *The Civil War Source Book* (New York, NY, 1992)

Katcher, Philip, *Great Gambles of the Civil War* (London, 1996)

Long, E.B., *The Civil War Day by Day* (Garden City, NJ, 1971)

Longstreet, James P., *From Manassas to Appomattox* (New York, NY, 1882). Reprinted 1991

McClellan, H.B., *The Campaigns of Stuart's Cavalry* (Secausus, NJ, 1993)

Moore, Frank (ed.), *Rebellion Record* (New York, NY, 1861–73). Eleven volumes

Newton, Steven H., *The Battle of Seven Pines, May 31–June 1, 1862* (Lynchburg, VA, 1993)

Robertson, James I. Jr., *Civil War Sites in Virginia* (Charlotteville, VA, 1982)

Sears, Stephen W., *George B. McClellan: The Young Napoleon* (New York, NY, 1988)

Sears, Stephen W., *To the Gates of Richmond: The Peninsular Campaign* (New York, NY, 1992)

Sibley, F. Ray, Jr., *The Confederate Order of Battle: The Army of Northern Virginia* (Shippensburg, PA, 1995)

Swinton, William, *Campaigns of the Army of the Potomac* (Secaucus, NJ, 1988)

Symonds, Craig L., *A Battlefield Atlas of the Civil War* (Baltimore, MD, 1983)

Thomason Jr., John W., *Jeb Stuart* (New York, NY, 1929). Reprinted by Bison Press (Lincoln, NE, 1994)

Underwood, Robert, and Buel, Clarence Clough (eds.), *Battles & Leaders of the Civil War* (Century Company, New York, NY, 1887). Four volumes. Reprinted by Castle (Edison, NJ, 1987). Note that this source contains articles originally published in Century Magazine. Volume II (*The Struggle Intensifies*) contains articles pertinent to the campaign

Warner, Ezra J., *Generals in Gray* (Baton Rouge, LA, 1959)

Wheeler, Richard, *Sword over Richmond: An eyewitness history of McClellan's Peninsular Campaign* (New York, NY, 1986)

Wise, Jennings Cropper, *The Long Arm of Lee* (New York, NY, 1991). Two volumes. Reprint of the 1915 edition

US Government Printing Office, *The War of the Rebellion: A Compilation of the Official Records of the Union & Confederate Armies* (Washington D.C., 1889–91). Seventy volumes. Series 1, Volume IX, Part II is pertinent to the campaign.

US Surgeon General's Office, *Medical & Surgical History of the War of the Rebellion* (Washington, D.C., 1875-1883). Three volumes

INDEX